DATE DUE

~~MAY 24~~			
~~MY 25 05~~			

DEMCO 38-296

KEY QUESTIONS IN CAREER COUNSELING
Techniques to Deliver Effective Career Counseling Services

KEY QUESTIONS IN CAREER COUNSELING
Techniques to Deliver Effective Career Counseling Services

Janice M. Guerriero, Ph.D.
Robert Glenn Allen, J.D., MBA

 LAWRENCE ERLBAUM ASSOCIATES, PUBLISHERS
1998   Mahwah, New Jersey   London

Lawrence Erlbaum Associates, Inc., Publishers
10 Industrial Avenue
Mahwah, New Jersey 07430

Cover Design by Kathryn Houghtaling Lacey

Library of Congress Cataloging-in-Publication-Data

Guerriero, Janice M.
Key questions in career counseling : techniques to deliver
effective career counseling services / Janice M. Guerriero, Robert
Glenn. Allen.
        p. cm.
    Includes index.
    ISBN 0-8058-3000-6 (alk. paper). — ISBN 0-8058-3001-4
(pbk. : alk. paper)
    1. Vocational guidance.   2. Counseling.   I. Allen, Robert
Glenn II. Title.
    HF5381.G8858   1998
    331.7'02—dc21   97-47701
                                                         CIP

Books published by Lawrence Erlbaum Associates are printed
on acid-free paper, and their bindings are chosen for strength
and durability.

Printed in the United States of America
10 9 8 7 6 5 4 3 2 1

Daniel Robert Nolan
May 8, 1996—May 30, 1996

A little child, here for
    such a short while,
Held our hearts; a
    tear, a smile,
But what great energy
    and resolve he gave
To our little project;
    so young, so brave.

Contents

About the Authors

Janice M. Guerriero is a management consultant, career counselor, and therapist in private practice. Her clients include employees of corporations, institutions, and firms, and self-referred individuals. Guerriero specializes in the use of assessment tools to provide a source of objective data within a program of service.

Among her degrees and credentials are: a Ph.D. in higher education, Wayne State University, Detroit, Michigan; master's in guidance and counseling, Oakland University, Rochester, Michigan; bachelor's in liberal arts, University of Michigan, Ann Arbor, Michigan; national certified counselor; national certified career counselor; certified alcohol and drug abuse counselor; certified social worker; and licensed clinical professional counselor.

Prior to the last 13 years of consulting and clinical work, Guerriero spent 9 years teaching at Oakland University in Rochester, Michigan. She taught counseling and internship courses in both a graduate program (guidance and counseling) and an undergraduate program (human resources development).

Guerriero is a member of the International Association of Career Management Professionals, the American/Illinois Counseling Associations, and the National/Illinois Career Development Associations.

Robert Glenn Allen is a director in the Baxter Institute for Training and Development for Baxter Healthcare Corporation, Deerfield, Illinois. He has corporatewide responsibility for career services, manages an account team, and delivers consulting and training in the areas of career development, leadership, teamwork, managing change, and strategic planning.

Prior to joining Baxter, Allen worked for Container Corporation of America in a variety of division and corporate employee relations positions, including director of headquarters human resources, corporate director of equal employment opportunity, and corporate director of compensation. He also worked for Mainstream Access, a human resources consulting firm, as senior managing consultant.

Allen received both a bachelor of arts degree in economics and a master's of business administration from the University of Kansas, Lawrence, Kansas, and he received a doctor of jurisprudence from the University of Texas School of Law, Austin, Texas.

Allen served on the board of directors of the International Association of Career Management Professionals and on the board of directors of the Private Industry Council of Northern Cook County, Illinois.

Guerriero and Allen are also the designers and facilitators of a three-level career counseling training program. These workshops have been conducted in corporate headquarters for both in-house groups and for open enrollment. As authors of the workshop training manuals, Guerriero and Allen field-tested the career counseling process model and key question materials in these workshops.

Preface

What could be better than having people ask you to write a book? What could be nicer than having workshop participants take notes on your ad libs? How about finding a compatible writing partner who balances your style, moods, and stamina? Yes, it is true, you may be lucky enough to leave your legacy in print, but, until you try it, you have no idea how to compress what you think you know about a subject into a useable tool for your intended audience.

We believe the work of career counseling requires both a "technology" and spontaneous imagination. We have provided a structured model as our technology and key questions to stimulate the imagination. We hope you can use some or all of our method to provide high-quality, effective career counseling services for your clients and yourself.

Acknowledgments

We would like to acknowledge the many supporters of our book project: Patricia Crull, our former vice president, who endorsed the development of the career counseling workshops; all the wonderful people at the Baxter Institute for Training and Development; the enthusiastic participants in the career counseling workshops who demanded more and more key questions; Cindy Kivland, our Consulting Psychologists Press representative, who threw the book idea at us; our colleagues and fellow IACMP members who cheered us on during the draft stages; Audrey Allen and extended family for giving up Bob on nights and weekends; the Guerriero clan, a family of firsts; Laurie Knutson, who persevered through numerous drafts with humor and patience; Jenny Harbecke, the fastest learner of software in the Midwest; and would-be authors out there—don't give up your dreams of being in print!

Inspiration

We were inspired by the model in Gottman and Leiblum's (1974) important work, *How To Do Psychotherapy and How to Evaluate It.*

A Very Special Thanks

A very special thanks goes to our first reviewers: David P. Meyer, Luellen Ramey, Angelo Guerriero, and Barbara Tartaglione. We appreciate their knowledge of the field; their fine editorial instincts; and their hearty encouragement. They will see their suggestions on the pages that follow.

—Janice M. Guerriero
—Robert Glenn Allen

Chapter 1

Introduction

Who Needs a Book on Techniques for Delivering Effective Career Counseling Services?

This book was written for people whose job responsibilities include, or will soon include, career advising, employee development, performance improvement, organizational planning, and outplacement. Examples of people with these responsibilities are:

- Managers and supervisors responsible for employee development, coaching, and performance evaluations.
- Human resources staff, especially those in planning, staffing, recruiting, and developing functions.
- Trainers and learning organization staff.
- Internal career advisors, coaches, and consultants.
- Adjunct consultants in career centers.
- Employee assistance program (EAP) staff.
- Outplacement consultants.
- School, college, and agency guidance counselors and placement personnel.
- Independent career counselors.

What Factors Are Driving the Need for Effective Career Counseling Services in the Workplace?

Factors leading to the need for competent career counseling services include these trends:

- Years of recessionary economy, devastating competition, massive downsizing, and increasing unemployment have created an unprecedented need for people to manage their own careers.
- Changing trade laws, deregulation, and global expansion have changed the types of jobs now needed to drive the marketplace.
- Rapidly changing technologies mean acquiring new skill sets faster than ever before.
- The increase in single-parent families and dual-career couples has created a demand for nontraditional work hours and work styles. The need for balancing family and work demands is greater than ever before.
- Baby boomers are the largest group of workers ever to reach retirement age in the same generation.

What Are the Consequences of These Factors on the Demand for Career Counseling Services?

Brown[1] capably discussed a variety of trends in career development. Some of his predictions that will impact career counselors and job seekers alike are:

- Technology has escalated career concerns. Workers must consider additional skills training and continuing education if they want to stay competitive in the marketplace.
- Job stress and lengthy unemployment are having an increasing impact on mental health. More workers are seeking both career counseling and personal counseling in an effort to regain control over their lives.
- More forms, settings, and types of career counseling services are beginning to emerge.
- Credentialing for career counselors is becoming more available. Graduate programs, certification, state licensing, and in-house training are aimed at professionalizing the practice of career counseling.
- Career counseling is becoming more like strategic planning. Those who are trying to meet the needs of a workforce in transition must quickly facilitate the identification of the career problem and then

[1]Brown, D. (1990). "Issues and trends in career development: Theory and practice." In D. Brown & L. Brooks (Eds.), *Career choice and development* (2nd ed., pp. 506–517). San Francisco: Jossey-Bass.

work with the client to develop the ability to be a better lifelong career planner.

- As baby boomers approach retirement age, they will seek creative ways to keep working. Career counselors will be needed to help this generation continue working after the traditional retirement age.
- Diversity issues will continue to dominate, as subgroups identify their own special career issues and solutions.
- Workers must adjust to technology and methodology or else productivity and quality will be adversely affected. Incentives in the form of career ladders and lattices will be available; career counselors will be needed to help guide workers through these choices.
- Career decision-making models will be a main feature of career counseling programs; workers who are risk-averse will not survive unless they learn effective ways of making the necessary changes.

What Is the Status of Career Counseling Services in the Workplace?

Quality of life and the balance between career and home life will dominate workers' priorities during the next decade. Many workers, such as those with entrepreneurial ambitions, will drop out of the traditional workforce. Young people coming into the workforce will be from a new generation with new value systems. Longevity and loyalty will be replaced by flextime, job sharing, home officing, contract employees, and the "virtual" office. All types of workers are likely to need the services of a career counselor to prepare them for these new realities.

Industries with the most job consistency and longevity, such as heavy manufacturing and engineering, have traditionally had the least need for career services. With the advancement of robotics and functional specialization, these industries are now seeking a new breed of manager: the technical team leader with people management skills. These developments reinforce the need for career counseling services in "mid-technology" occupations.

Some industries are growing in a healthy way and seek to develop their existing workforce. Examples are hotel and food industries and consumer products. Career counseling will be needed to guide employees toward a good fit between their aptitudes and newly developed jobs.

High-tech organizations typically recruit or promote talent as fast as their technology expands. High-tech industries are underserved by career counselors because recruiters tend to be the point of contact in these fast-moving organizations.

Schools and universities, nonprofit organizations, and government agencies all have placement needs, depending on funding levels, projected service needs, and available talent. Because the hiring process is slow and frequently stalled, career counseling becomes even more important to workers wishing to advance.

What Are the Development Needs of Career Counseling Practitioners?

Anyone with responsibility for delivering career counseling services should be trained to use a process or sequential model containing the stages of career counseling. Academically trained career counselors might use such a model, but most career counselors trained on the job do not. There are large numbers of career counselors who have no process-oriented training. They rely on exercises, problem solving, and job-search coaching more than on assessment, planning, and client self-management.

What Are Some of the Benefits of Learning and Applying a Career Counseling Process Model?

There are numerous advantages in using a process model:

- Managers will have a uniform model to ensure consistent service delivery and client satisfaction.
- Practitioners will have a sequential model for accomplishing the tasks of career counseling.
- Practitioners and clients will be able to proceed more effectively through the counseling process by using uniform tools and resources.
- Clients will become more self-reliant by using the stages and steps of the model to manage their careers.

How Can This Book Help Career Counseling Practitioners to Develop a Higher Skill Level?

Here are some of the ways in which this book can develop career counselors' capabilities:

- Readers will learn a logical, step-by-step model for conducting career counseling.
- The model shows the sequence of steps to use in order to help clients develop and implement strategic career action plans.
- The model shows how to move through the beginning, middle, and end of the career counseling stages and how to achieve closure.
- Readers will receive tools to help evaluate their effectiveness as career counselors.

The model is activated by the use of key questions asked during each of its stages and steps. Once these key questions are learned, career counselors will be much more effective and empowering with their clients.

How Will the Model and Key Questions Be Demonstrated in the Book?

To demonstrate how to use the model and the key questions technique, vignettes have been placed throughout the book. The vignettes are brief stories in which the key questions are applied to whatever stage and steps are presented in the chapter. The vignettes track the progress of a fictitious client "Mary H." Mary's career counseling episodes appear in chapters 4 through 9, from the foundation stage through the follow-through stage of the career counseling model.

How Can the Learning in This Book Be Reinforced?

At the end of each chapter is a section called learning reinforcement. Each learning reinforcement has three parts: terms and definitions, review questions, and additional resources. The terms and definitions and review

questions will help career counselors recall the most important new learning
in each chapter. The additional resources provide a guide to further reading
and research on the chapter topics.

What Career Counseling Tools Are Available in the Book?

The appendices contain the tools mentioned in each chapter, such as the
career counseling process model, the career counseling process handout,
exercises, inventories, questionnaires, career data forms, and publisher
sources.

Chapter 2

The Career Counseling Process Model

Effective career counseling depends on a number of factors, including the use of a process that helps a client address his or her particular career needs. It is important that the counselor understands what the process is, how it can be used, and what is particularly unique about the specific stages and steps of the process.

As the process is explained, many key questions are introduced. These questions serve as a bridge between the process model and the daily work of counseling clients.

There are several terms that should be understood in order to better follow the various stages of the process.

What Is a Process?   A process is a number of sequential steps that need to be taken in order to complete a given task or to produce a result. It might be helpful to view a process as a way of achieving an output or creating a product. In career counseling, a series of steps are taken with the objective of creating a strategic career action plan.

The first step in the career counseling process requires *inputs*, such as interview responses, records, and work history.

The next step in the process is called the *transformational* step, an action that converts the information. In career counseling, this is normally the interpretation of the information that has been collected.

The third step in the process is the *output*, or the results of the transformation of the raw materials. In career counseling, this product is an action plan that the candidate implements to reach his or her specific career goal.

What Is a Model?   A model is an explanation of how something is supposed to work. It is a picture of how various elements fit together. A model can be used to track the order of operations or it can be adjusted to meet given circumstances. For example, one stage in the career counseling process is called *assessment*. During this stage, one step is selecting and administering assessment tools. If recent tests have been completed, this assessment step may be skipped.

If something goes wrong during implementation of a process, the model can be referred to in order to determine why the trouble occurred. It might be a missing part of the process or a lost step. The culprit might be contaminated data. Having a model to follow helps the user locate the missing parts.

Referring to the process model is like looking at a "blueprint." If there is a design to which a builder can refer, it is much more likely that the building will be built correctly and that high-quality structures will be consistently built. Similarly, career counseling can be done correctly and with high quality by adhering to a process and using a model, or blueprint, to ensure that counselors are on the right track.

Career counseling is a process with inputs, transformations, and outputs. The career counseling model, or blueprint, shows how the process should work.

Why Use a Career Counseling Process Model?   The career counseling process model contains a sequence of stages for obtaining career information, analyzing or interpreting it, and creating goals and action plans. It provides the structure within which the counselor and the client play identified roles of helper and helpee and work together according to certain time frames and organizational expectations. The career counseling process model is developmental, that is, the elementary stages have to come before the intermediate and advanced stages.

It has been shown that human growth and maturation occur in evolving developmental stages. So do career growth and maturation. It is not unusual for stages to be skipped; but if they are skipped in a developmental model, a person will probably have to go back and pick up the missing pieces in order to create the proper foundation for later stages.

Career advisors may have asked themselves:

- Are there steps or stages in career counseling, and if so, what are they?
- How am I supposed to conduct the sessions?
- Where do I begin?
- How do I know if I'm doing it right?

- What do I do if I/we get stuck?
- How do I know when we are finished?
- What is successful career counseling?

The career counseling process model and key questions will help career advisors answer these questions.

A Note About Career Development Theories. There are many books and articles detailing various theories of career development. Some of these theories have related models and techniques for the practice of career counseling. Because these resources are plentiful and exist elsewhere, we have chosen not to repeat the specifics of those theories in this publication. We have listed some appropriate sources in the additional resources section at the end of this chapter.

We recommend that those unfamiliar with career development theories read one or more of the selections listed to enhance professional development and reinforce the use of any model of career counseling practice.

Presentation of the Model

It is important to understand the various stages of the model, how the process flows from one stage to another, and how to use the model.

The Six Stages of the Career Counseling Process Model. There are six stages in the model: foundation, assessment, feedback, goal setting, resistance resolution, and follow through. Figure 2.1 depicts the six stages.

During the *foundation stage*, the counselor clarifies how the client was referred for service; why the client is presently seeking career help; and what roles and tasks are expected of the counselor and client.

During the *assessment stage*, pertinent data are collected via documents, interviews, observation, resume, referring source, and so on. A career or job history is obtained. Assessment instruments may be administered and a career data profile developed.

During the *feedback stage*, the counselor presents data profiles or themes to the client. Patterns and cycles are validated. Conclusions drawn from the data will be used to develop the career plan.

During the *goal-setting stage*, the counselor and client outline career options and establish priorities. A preliminary action plan can be drafted, based on the client's skills, knowledge, and experience, plus existing market conditions and environmental factors. In addition, the plan is tested to assess its viability.

During the *resistance resolution stage*, obstacles to plan implementation are identified, sources of the obstacles are addressed, resistance is resolved, and the client is linked to appropriate resources.

The *follow-through stage* is crucial to successful outcomes. There should be checkpoints during the plan in case revisions need to be made. After service has ended, the client should be able to maintain the process or have access to other help. Aspects of the counseling, such as counselor effective-

FIG. 2.1. Career counseling process model.	
I. THE FOUNDATION STAGE	
FIRST STEP	UNDERSTAND THE REFERRAL
	• Determine how the client was referred for counseling.
SECOND STEP	DETERMINE THE PRECIPITATING EVENT
	• Why is career counseling being sought now?
	• Elicit candidate concerns and expectations.
	• Be sensitive to cross-cultural and diversity issues.
	• Determine if third-party consultation will occur with the client's manager, HR liaison, or other resource people.
THIRD STEP	EXPLAIN THE CAREER COUNSELING PROCESS
	• Explain the process and roles of counselor and client.
	• Develop the counselor–client relationship.
↓	
II. THE ASSESSMENT STAGE	
FIRST STEP	IDENTIFY CLIENT CAREER CONCERNS
	• What are the two or three career questions the client would like to have answered during the counseling?
SECOND STEP	OBTAIN A CAREER HISTORY
	• Collect as much information as possible about a client's career history.
THIRD STEP	SELECT AND ADMINISTER ASSESSMENT TOOLS
	• Determine if inventories and standardized career tests would complement the career history.
FOURTH STEP	INTERPRET THE ASSESSMENT DATA
	• Analyze patterns in assessment results and compare with existing data. Explain consistencies or inconsistencies.
FIFTH STEP	CREATE A CAREER DATA PROFILE
	• Summarize the assessment data on a chart.

	⬇
	III. THE FEEDBACK STAGE
FIRST STEP	PROCESS INTERVIEW AND ASSESSMENT FINDINGS • Determine if the findings fit the client's perceptions. • Find out how the client feels about the results.
SECOND STEP	VALIDATE PATTERNS OR CYCLES • Help the client take ownership of the findings.
THIRD STEP	LINK CONCLUSIONS TO CLIENT QUESTIONS • Connect data outcomes to changes the client will be expected to make.
FOURTH STEP	OUTLINE CAPABILITIES AND AREAS FOR ACTION • Create a list of actions that will meet the needs of the client and the employer/job market.
	⬇
	IV. THE GOAL-SETTING STAGE
FIRST STEP	OUTLINE CAREER OPTIONS • List all options supported by the assessment stage.
SECOND STEP	ESTABLISH PRIORITIES • Rank the options in order of highest desirability, or highest probability of success.
THIRD STEP	DRAFT A PRELIMINARY CAREER GOAL • Determine the goal best supported by the preceding stages and steps.
FOURTH STEP	DRAFT A STRATEGIC CAREER ACTION PLAN • Document in detail an overall plan of action, including an obstacle analysis and a timeline for implementation.
FIFTH STEP	GAIN CLIENT COMMITMENT • Ensure that the client designed the plan and has the power to execute it.
	⬇
	V. THE RESISTANCE RESOLUTION STAGE
FIRST STEP	IDENTIFY CONFLICTS OR IMPASSES TO IMPLEMENTATION OF THE ACTION PLAN • Determine if the client is aware of blocks to implementing the strategic career action plan.
SECOND STEP	ASSESS THE SOURCE(S) OF RESISTANCE • Is the client fighting change (risk-averse)? • Does the client lack certain capabilities (knowledge, skills, or traits)? • Are there blocking factors in the work environment? • Is there a problem with the counselor or the counseling process?

THIRD STEP	RESOLVE RESISTANCE USING TOOLS AND INTERVENTIONS
	• Use appropriate exercises and didactic materials to reduce or eliminate the resistance.
FOURTH STEP	LINK CLIENT TO APPROPRIATE RESOURCES FOR IMPLEMENTATION
	• Identify appropriate people, information, financial resources, and experiential opportunities to ensure implementation of the strategic career action plan.

⬇

VI. THE FOLLOW-THROUGH STAGE

FIRST STEP	TRANSFER RESPONSIBILITY TO THE CLIENT
	• Client takes over the tasks of career planning and management.
SECOND STEP	MONITOR PROGRESS IN THE IMPLEMENTATION OF THE STRATEGIC CAREER ACTION PLAN
	• Identify check points that coincide with the timeline in the plan.
THIRD STEP	ACKNOWLEDGE CLOSURE OF THE COUNSELING RELATIONSHIP AND THE FORMAL COUNSELING PROGRAM
	• Agree that the formal program and relationship has come to an end.
FOURTH STEP	EVALUATE THE EFFECTIVENESS OF THE CAREER COUNSELING
	• Facilitate closure by measuring the value of the service, the counselor skills, and the client's readiness.
FIFTH STEP	DESIGN ADDITIONAL INTERVENTIONS IF NECESSARY
	• Determine if re-entering or starting a new career counseling program is appropriate.

ness, program deliverables, and client satisfaction, should be evaluated for continuous improvement.

Using the Career Counseling Process Model. An ideal time sequence for all 6 stages, which include 26 steps, would be to have six to eight meetings with a career client, each lasting 60 to 90 minutes. However, the model can be adjusted to fit the environment in which career counselors work. Once counselors understand the logic in the progressive steps, they can compress the steps in order to meet restricted time limits. For example, if there are only one or two meetings with a client, data, such as resumes, performance reports, or test data can be obtained in advance. In addition, counselors can assign pre-work exercises, communicate by phone, assign homework between sessions, and use strategic action plan forms to help deal with system or time constraints. Follow-up is sometimes done by phone, fax, or mail.

Chapter Summary

The career counseling process model has 6 stages and 26 steps within the stages. It is driven by key questions and subquestions that help the counselor and the client move through the process. The model is in the form of a flowchart. Within the flowchart is a stage for analyzing and resolving resistance to achieving the client's career goals.

Learning Reinforcement

1. Terms and Definitions
   a. *Process*: A process is a series of steps taken to complete a task and produce a result.
   b. *Model*: A model is an explanation of how something should work. It is like a blueprint that shows how the parts fit together.
   c. *Career Counseling Process Model*: This model is a sequence of stages and steps for obtaining career information, analyzing or interpreting it, and creating goals and action plans.
   d. *Developmental Model*: A developmental model is a growth model. It has elementary stages that come before intermediate and advanced stages.
2. Review Questions
   a. What is a process model?
   b. What are the six stages in the career counseling process model?
   c. What is the purpose of each stage?
   d. When might a modified version of this model be used?
3. Additional Resources
   a. Brown, D., & Brooks, L. (1990). *Career choice and development.* San Francisco: Jossey-Bass.
   b. Geldard, D. (1989). *Basic personal counseling.* Springfield, IL: Charles C. Thomas.
   c. Isaacson, L. E. (1985). *Basics of career counseling.* Boston: Allyn & Bacon.
   d. Ivey, A. E., & Authier, J. (1978). *Microcounseling* (2nd ed.). Springfield, IL: Charles C. Thomas.

e. Lea, H.D., & Leibowitz, Z. B. (1992). *Adult career development: Concepts, issues, and practices.* Alexandria, VA: National Career Development Association.

f. McDaniels, C., & Gysbers, N. (1992). *Counseling for career development.* San Francisco: Jossey-Bass.

g. Sharf, R. S. (1997). *Applying career development theory to counseling.* Pacific Grove, CA: Brooks/Cole.

h. Stewart, N. R., Winhorn, B. B., Johnson, R. G., Burks, H. M., Jr., & Engelkes, J. R. (1978). *Systematic counseling.* Englewood Cliffs, NJ: Prentice-Hall.

i. Stoltz-Loike, M. (1996). Annual review: Practice and research in career development and counseling–1995. *The Career Development Quarterly, 45,* 99–140.

j. Super, D. E., Osborne, W. L., Walsh, D. J., Brown, S. D., & Niles, S. G. (1992). Developmental career assessment and counseling: The C-ADC model. *Journal of Counseling and Development, 71,* 549–554.

k. Yost, E. B., & Corbishley, M. A. (1987). *Career counseling, a psychological approach.* San Francisco: Jossey-Bass.

l. Zunker, V. G. (1990). *Using assessment results for career development.* Pacific Grove, CA: Brooks/Cole.

Chapter 3

The Key Questions Technique

Key questions are primarily used to gather data and to facilitate the movement of the client through the career counseling process. Instead of talking about general unemployment problems, the state of the economy, the mismanagement of the company, and so on, counselors and their clients seek information about the client's specific career experiences. For example, if a client says, "I'll never get promoted with the boss I've got," a counselor might ask the following questions:

- Have you been turned down recently for a promotion?
- When was your last promotion?
- Are there promotions now available in your group/team/organization?
- What is your promotion history, and how did you obtain the promotions before?

Some further key questions might be:

- Is this how you feel about your current boss, or any boss?
- What kind of work do you feel has promotional possibilities for you?

Other uses of key questions are to identify and clarify issues that need to be addressed and to uncover some of the answers to the overall career question.

The Art of Using Key Questions

Most career counselors probably have already created and used dozens of effective key questions. A question is a "key" question if it enhances the career exploration and sheds new light on the problem. It may be necessary to ask several related key questions to stimulate a client's imagination. One result of using a good key question is the solution focus. Examples of solution-focused key questions are as follows:

- We have three sessions in which to develop a strategic career action plan. How can we make the most effective use of our time?
- What attempts have you made already to change your job responsibilities, and how successful were you?
- What is your time frame for finding another job?
- Whom do you include in your support system and are they available to brainstorm solutions with you?
- How long will it take you to draft a resume?

Another result of using key questions is the exploration of issues related to career development. Examples of these questions are:

- What sorts of activities give you the most satisfaction?
- What are some examples of situations in which you have been particularly uncomfortable?

The art of using key questions is based on the ability to link the questions in some way to the career problem. An example is a case in which a client expresses a lot of interest in changing to a career in advertising. A counseling goal would be to see if there is a skills/experience fit. Some key questions might be:

- How did you become interested in advertising?
- Have any of your previous jobs been related to advertising?
- What are your transferable skills to the field of advertising?
- Do you have friends, family members, or neighbors working in advertising?
- What would be some quick ways of learning about jobs and salaries for newcomers in advertising?

The questions are drawn from the career problem, which was "Could this client make a successful transition to a career in advertising?"

Sometimes clients do not understand initial key questions because they are not used to questioning methods or because they do not understand certain terms. More specific, detail-focused key questions allow counselors to pursue one topic more deeply, with the hope of triggering some choices from the client. Taking one of the key questions from the previous paragraph, here are some follow-up key questions directed at a deeper level of detail:

Counselor: *Have any of your previous jobs been related to advertising?* (initial key question)

Client: *What do you mean?*

Counselor: *Your resume indicates you have data entry, clerical, purchasing, and customer service experience primarily in small manufacturing and contracting businesses. Did any of these companies have advertising departments or use advertising firms, and were you assigned any responsibilities where you learned about advertising?*

Client: *I have studied advertising in college, as well as consumer psychology and sociology. If I ever finish my degree, then I could get a job in advertising.*

Counselor: *How close are you to finishing a degree that could help qualify you for a position in advertising?*

Client: *I have been going to night school for 6 years; I'm working on my associate's degree. I think I will major in business.*

Counselor: *What are some activities, such as a company newsletter, or a United Way campaign, for which you could volunteer?*

Client: *I see what you're getting at. Maybe there's something I can do in my present job that will give me writing or public relations experience.*

In this example, through the use of detailed key questions, the counselor helped the client discover connections between his or her skills and experiences and the requirements of a desirable job.

Key Questions Create Awareness and Change

When people are in unfamiliar territory, or under a lot of stress, they tend to forget the wisdom they have accumulated over the years. People in crisis or under pressure often revert to old ways of thinking instead of availing themselves of new possibilities. Asking key questions can help a client connect with the deeper reasons for the counseling. Key questions heighten a client's awareness of the need for change. The counselor's role is not to provide all the answers to the client's career questions, but to facilitate the client's answers to the key questions.

Key Questions Lead to Solutions

One of the strongest human drives is the desire for closure. Counselors can utilize this need to solve the career problem. Here is an example of how a counselor helped a client reach closure:

Counselor: *You are at loose ends because a merger of your company is about to take place and you don't know if or when your position will be eliminated. How have you handled other unknowns like this in the past, and how did things work out for you?*

Client: *You're right. I hate waiting. We had a restructuring 4 years ago, and our jobs were up in the air for almost 7 months. We couldn't concentrate on our work because all of a sudden our function was unneeded by the company. I was so upset I had to go to the employee assistance office and talk to a therapist.*

Counselor: *What did you find out by talking to the therapist?*

Client: *Actually, it was kind of reassuring because the therapist helped me see that I was really worried about my spending habits and my mother's illness more than about losing my job. I have good skills. I can get another job. But it will be expensive if I have to relocate, and I can't leave my mother.*

Counselor: *You did the right thing by talking to a therapist. What you have here are three separate but interrelated issues: potential job loss, spending more than you can afford, and the responsibility of taking care of your mother. What did you do regarding employment after the last restructuring?*

Client: *I was willing to take a lateral move and take on some additional responsibilities. I wanted to learn more computer skills anyway, and that's exactly what happened. I am now an expert user of database and spreadsheet programs. In fact, I bet I could teach these software applications to the newcomers because they haven't had access to the software that we do.*

Counselor: *You seem somewhat more confident about your options now that you have recalled your past coping responses.*

Client: *That's true. I have been able to adjust to big changes before by looking for hidden opportunities.*

By using key questions on job-related themes, the counselor and the client concluded that effective strategies from the past probably could be applied to the present concerns.

Managing the Use of Key Questions

Before the use of key questions is undertaken in career counseling work, counselors should think about how they would react to this technique as clients. They would want to have adequate rapport and trust with the counselor, they would want stimulating questions, and they would want to be challenged at a reasonable pace. As a counselor, managing the use of key questions means having built the necessary rapport and trust with clients by carefully explaining the roles and responsibilities in the career counseling process and by assuring confidentiality for each client.

Additionally, counselors need to be selective and appropriate about which questions to ask, rather than using irrelevant questions just because they are in the book. They should avoid becoming interrogators. They should pace themselves and listen carefully to their clients' responses. Follow-up questions should be directly linked to the clients' original career questions and stated goals. Counselors should remember that key questions that would work well with themselves probably will work well with their clients. Likewise, a pace or focus that counselors would not like would not be appreciated if they imposed it on their clients.

Chapter Summary

Key questions are extremely useful in helping the client stay focused on career issues. Often, initial key questions need to be followed by more probing key questions. These questions are particularly useful when used in tandem with the stages and steps in the career counseling process. Key questions help the counselor and the client identify solutions to the career problem.

The next six chapters contain explanations of the stages and steps in the career counseling process model, key questions for each stage and step in the model, and a case study showing how to apply the model and key questions. As a learning aid and reference tool, readers may refer to Appendix A. The checklist provided there contains all the key questions for each stage and step mentioned throughout the book.

Learning Reinforcement

1. Terms and Definitions
   a. *Initial Key Questions*: Initial key questions are solution-oriented questions used to obtain data needed to solve the career problem.
   b. *Follow-up Key Questions*: Follow-up key questions are detailed questions that are used after initial key questions to clarify data, explore a subject in more detail, or trigger new career choices.
2. Review Questions
   a. What is the formula for creating key questions?
   b. What is the purpose of follow-up key questions?
   c. How does the use of questions lead to solutions?
   d. What are some examples of key questions that might be used in career counseling?
3. Additional Resources
   a. Merman, E. K., & McLaughlin, J. F. (1983). *Out-interviewing the interviewer*. Englewood Cliffs, NJ: Prentice-Hall.
   b. Stewart, C. J., & Cash, W. B. (1982). *Interviewing: Principles and practices*. Dubuque, IA: Wm. C. Brown.

Chapter 4

The Foundation Stage

As discussed in chapter 2, there are six stages in the career counseling process. Each stage has its own particular purpose and key questions.

The first stage is the foundation stage, the beginning point in the process. This stage is critical to ensuring that the career counseling outcomes are meaningful and meet the expectations of the various stakeholders. There are three steps in the foundation stage: understand the referral, determine the precipitating event, and explain the career counseling process.

These steps ensure that there is mutual understanding and agreement about how the client will benefit from career counseling. It is during the foundation stage that the counselor and the client establish a comfortable pace, which adds to the necessary rapport to proceed through the other stages of the career counseling process. Care should be taken by counselors not to get caught up in simply going through the stages checklist (Appendix A). The career counseling process model and its key questions were designed to inspire a dialogue of trust. Through this dialogue, it is possible to deepen the impact and ultimate effectiveness of a client's career objectives.

Key Questions: The Foundation Stage

The three overall key questions that drive the foundation stage are:

- What are the expected outcomes?
- What counseling has occurred before?
- Do you understand the career counseling process?

Step 1: Understand the Referral

At the beginning of the foundation stage the career counselor needs to be absolutely sure that he or she fully understands the referral. Every client has one or more reasons for seeking career counseling. The client may be totally or only somewhat aware of these reasons. If the client is being sponsored by an employer, some of the reasons for counseling may be hidden or only partially clarified. It is the counselor's responsibility to be sure that the reasons are "on the table" for all to see. Without clarity around expectations, the counseling is potentially doomed for failure.

More key questions for Step 1 are:

- What are your reasons for seeking career counseling?
- Do all parties agree that this is why we are working together?
- If there is not total agreement, what do you need to do so that all parties are in agreement?

In addition to clarifying the expectations, the counselor will be contracting with the client regarding roles, expectations, confidentiality, expected results, time frames, follow-up, and so on. Useful key questions for contracting include:

- What are your expectations?
- How did you decide to seek career counseling?
- Who else knows that we are meeting? Did they tell you what they want you to accomplish?
- How are the fees for the services going to be paid?
- Have you ever been involved in career counseling before? If so, what were the outcomes?
- Do you have any copies of previous career counseling assessment materials, action plans, etc.?
- Do you have a time limitation or deadline for completing the counseling?
- When we are finished, what is the final product going to look like?

Vignette

Mary H. has been sent to you for counseling. All you know is that she has been authorized to receive 8 hours of counseling and that there are "performance issues." By asking the preceding key questions, you learn that Mary is hopeful of "getting out of my situation." She is willing to work on her development needs, but down deep she believes that a transfer to another job is the long-term solution to her situation. She has asked you to keep this fact confidential.

Her boss, Ellen F., has sent many people to you and wants a "well thought-out plan of action within a month or so." Mary's company will pay for the counseling. She has never received career counseling before, except for informal advice from human resources personnel and various supervisors.

Step 2: Determine the Precipitating Event

Once the referral and expectations have been clarified, the counselor should next determine the precipitating event. There is almost always one or more events that have prompted the client to seek counseling. The counselor needs to understand what has triggered the client to seek career counseling.

To understand the reasons behind the referral, the following key questions can be used:

- Why are you being sent to me now?
- Why are you here talking to me?
- If I were to ask your boss why we are working together, what would I be told?
- Is this a new situation or one that has been going on for some time?

By understanding the precipitating event, the counselor will be able to get a clearer understanding of any hidden concerns and expectations.

Additional key questions include:

- Do you view yourself as being in crisis? If so, what is your support system?
- Are you receiving (or have you received) any personal counseling from an employee assistance program counselor, private therapist, minister, etc.? If so, what can you share with me? If so, does this person know that you are meeting with me for career counseling?
- Do you have any sensitivities about your career, job search, career success, etc.? Do you have any concerns about this counseling?
- Are there any cultural issues? Anything tied to lifestyle, race, religion, etc.?

Vignette

You learn by using various key questions that Mary H. has just completed her yearly performance review and that this is the trigger for her visit with you. Previous performance ratings were reflective of "good" or "outstand-ing" performance. The most recent review resulted in a rating of "needs improvement." She is viewed by her boss as reactive instead of proactive, a poor team player, and not good at dealing with conflict.

Mary feels threatened and is fearful of losing her job and benefits coverage. She has never received counseling before, except for marriage counseling from her minister that began about 6 months ago. She hopes that her marriage problems are not viewed as a sign of weakness by her boss. She tells you that divorce is frowned upon by several of her fellow employees.

Step 3: Explain the Career Counseling Process

Having agreed on what is expected and having clarified the circumstances that resulted in seeking career counseling, it is important that the client fully understand the career counseling process.

The career counseling process can be explained in a variety of ways using both visual aids and verbal discussion. It is essential that the client under-stand each of the six stages in the process: foundation, assessment, feed-back, goal setting, resistance resolution, and follow through. A good method of explaining the process is to use the outline provided in Appendix B.

It should be explained that the counselor and the client are going to work together during a certain number of sessions to complete the outlined tasks. If additional time or services appear to be needed, the process will be re-evaluated as the need arises.

This explanation step in the process is an excellent opportunity to reinforce the counselor–client relationship. The counselor might say such things as "In the role of career counselor, I am your guide (sounding board/advocate/resource) for the career counseling process. Your role is to explore all your career options and to communicate how the process is progressing to those to whom you are accountable." Other instructions might include statements such as: "Our work is completely confidential, unless you ask me to provide others with specific career information during a three-way consultation" and "I do not provide job placement or personnel recommendations unless we agree that I have the authority to play that role and that it is part of our career counseling agenda."

After presenting the outline and the clarifications, a key question is, "Do you have any questions before we start?"

Chapter Summary

This completes the foundation stage of the career counseling process. The boundaries have been set by establishing the reasons for the referral, the expected results of the counseling, and what is going to occur during the various sessions. During the next stage, the assessment stage, the counselor and the client will be accumulating relevant career data in order to objectively evaluate the client's options.

Learning Reinforcement

1. Terms and Definitions
   a. *The Foundation Stage:* The foundation stage clarifies the referral, roles, and expectations for the counseling process.
   b. *Expectations*: Expectations are the anticipated results or deliverables that the various parties to the counseling desire at the end of the process.
2. Review Questions
   a. What are the three steps in the foundation stage?
   b. Why is it so important to determine the reason why the client is seeking career counseling?
   c. In addition to the precipitating event, what other information should you seek regarding the client's timing of the counseling?
   d. Why is it important to explain the career counseling process to the client?
3. Additional Resources
   a. Bolton, R. (1979). *People skills*. New York: Simon & Schuster.
   b. D'Andrea, V., & Salovey, P. (1983). *Peer counseling*. Palo Alto, CA: Science & Behavior.

Chapter 5

The Assessment Stage

The assessment stage can begin once the career issue has been defined, expectations have been clarified, and a counseling relationship has been established with the client. There are five steps in the assessment stage: identify client career concerns, obtain a career history, select and administer assessment tools, interpret the assessment data, and create a career data profile.

In the assessment stage, relevant career data, such as resumes, performance reviews, job descriptions, test results, and answers to interview questions are collected. Some career counselors use whatever documents are at hand. Others supplement basic information with career instruments such as the Campbell Interest and Skills Survey (CISS), the Holland Self-Directed Search (SDS), the Myers-Briggs Type Indicator (MBTI), and the Personal Profile System (PPS). There are many other career assessment measures (see the additional resources provided at the end of the chapter). Appendix C contains a list of popular career assessment materials and publishers. The use of career instruments depends on the amount and depth of career counseling to be conducted; the level of training, certification, and expertise of the counselor; and the policies and practices of the organization being served.

A good assessment contains information from many sources. A career advisor can help prepare a client for decision making by assembling the client's career history, written records, and, if appropriate, assessment results.

Key Questions: The Assessment Stage

The overall key questions that drive the assessment stage are:

- What career data do you have readily at hand?
- What information needs to be collected?
- What are the significant findings in the career data profile?

Step 1: Identify Client Career Concerns

During the foundation stage, one of the key objectives was to determine why the person is seeking career counseling and what is the career issue. At the beginning of the assessment stage, the first step is to determine what the client needs to know in order to resolve the career issue.

People seek career counseling for many reasons. They bring into the discussion a number of interlocking concerns: future career direction, performance expectations, co-worker conflicts, money issues, fear of job loss, and family stresses, to name just a few. The purpose of career counseling is to help a client make informed decisions from a number of options. A counselor can start the assessment stage by asking this key question:

- What two or three career questions would you like to have answered as a result of the career counseling?

The client's responses explain what he or she wants to take away from the sessions. If a client is not sure of how to answer this initial key question, there are some additional key questions counselors might use as prompts:

- Are there some unknowns regarding your skills, aptitudes, interests, or values?
- Have you received positive or negative feedback about your career choice that you don't agree with?
- Have you ever thought you would be happier in a different job/career/work environment?
- Have you been repeating some of the same employment mistakes or patterns?
- Three months from now, what would you like to see changed in your career?
- Are you managing your career or is it managing you?

Vignette

In the foundation stage, you were introduced to a fictitious client named Mary H. Mary has been sent to you by her boss, Ellen F. for 8 hours of performance-related counseling. Mary has asked you to keep confidential the fact that she is actually seeking a transfer to another job. She does understand that her boss is expecting a plan of action that will address Mary's performance deficiencies.

After noting both Mary's and Ellen's reasons for the referral, you used the career counseling process handout (Appendix B) to explain the stages and steps to Mary. Next you start the assessment stage by asking Mary what two or three career questions she would like to have answered. Mary wants to know what other jobs exist for which she is qualified, what she has to do to prepare for a transfer, and how she can leave her boss and present position without creating hard feelings. Mary admits that her confidence is at an all-time low after receiving a "needs improvement" performance rating and struggling with the possibility of divorce.

You point out to Mary that another career question that has to be answered during the counseling sessions is how she will address the performance issues and create a development plan to take back to her manager. She agrees with this fourth career question.

Step 2: Obtain a Career History

In order to fully understand a client's career needs, the counselor should collect as much information as possible about how the person's career has evolved. The first items to assemble are documents such as the client's resume, job descriptions, performance reviews, and school transcripts. Once these data are collected, the counselor needs to put whatever facts he or she has accumulated into a chronological career history. The client should be asked to describe the positives and negatives for each major career event. In some settings, clients receive feedback via upward or multisource feedback tools, or through team performance measures. If available, these reports might reveal some additional behavioral data that will be useful.

Some of the key questions to ask in obtaining a career history are:

- Could you provide me with your resume, your most recent job description, and any performance reviews you might have?
- What other job records do you have?
- For each of your jobs: What were your responsibilities? What did you like best about the job? What did you like least? What were your major accomplishments?
- What is your salary history?
- What were you trained for in school? In the armed forces? Tell me more.

- Have you had any on-the-job training? Tell me about it.
- What are your strongest job skills? Your weakest?
- Have you ever participated in any multisource feedback process? If so, do you have notes or reports?
- Have you participated in any workshops where co-workers were asked to give you feedback on communication style or team behaviors? What feedback did you receive?
- What career path have you been following?

Vignette

From Mary H.'s resume you learn that, in her present company, she has held a series of clerical support positions ranging from secretary to coordinator. Her previous work experience of 6 years included jobs in fast food restaurants, customer service, and office management.

Mary has a high school diploma with office skills and co-op credits and a 2-year degree in office practices from a community college. Her resume also lists many courses in wordprocessing, spreadsheet, and database software.

Mary's current job title is database coordinator. Her job description specifies strong organizational and planning skills, effective customer and team communication, and strong computer skills. As a member of a cross-departmental team, she collects and inputs data and distributes reports to all team members. She also handles requests from customers. Mary enjoys the positive feedback she gets from satisfying customers' needs. Her major dissatisfaction in the job occurs when she needs to work closely with a team member. There are disagreements over how something should be done.

Mary considers this position to be her most stressful job to date because of the volume of work, the competition among co-workers, and the demands of the team-oriented environment.

Her pattern has been to move from position to position when the pressure becomes too great. From her perspective, her best job experience was on a customer service hotline explaining product specifications and pricing to potential and existing customers.

Mary has received performance review feedback from Ellen F., her boss, stating that her behavior is reactive instead of proactive. She has been told that she is a poor team player and that she is not good at dealing with conflict.

Step 3: Select and Administer Assessment Tools

The client's career issues that were identified in Step 1 of the assessment stage should be an indication of whether assessment instruments would be helpful in career planning. Mary H.'s career questions were:

- What other jobs am I qualified for?
- What do I have to do to prepare for a transfer?
- How can I leave my present boss/position without hard feelings?

A fourth question was added as a result of the referral information from her boss:

- How will Mary address the performance issues and create a development plan to take back to her manager?

The first client career question pertains to skill sets. Because Mary has a tendency to change jobs frequently, it would be helpful to measure her skills and interests. Typical skills and interest measures are the CISS and the SDS.

The second client career question relates to job-search skills such as networking and researching positions. This question can be addressed by asking Mary about the process she used in her previous job searches.

The third client career question suggests that Mary H. is a person who is making job decisions without an overarching career plan. Her jobs are more like career skips than career steps. Instruments that reveal a person's communication style, preferences, and ideal role are the MBTI and the PPS. Both are useful in selecting good fit occupations.

The fourth client career question is about behavior change. Learning more about Mary H.'s temperament and interpersonal style will be useful in addressing the difference between her present behavior and the desired behavior. The MBTI and the PPS materials contain personal style and role descriptions, as well as specific remedies for addressing developmental needs.

Some key questions for Step 3 are:

- Have you ever completed any career or aptitude testing? If so, please bring copies of the scores or reports to our next session.

- Have you ever completed instruments for the purpose of clarifying your career goals and making better decisions? If so, can you bring copies to our next session?

Here are some additional key questions that can be used to supplement the use of the assessment instruments:

- What are your strongest skill sets?
- In what skill areas have you shown the most improvement over time?
- What job activities do you most enjoy?
- How do you spend most of your time on the job?
- What skills have you been able to teach others?
- What motivates you on the job?
- What demotivates you on the job?
- How do others see you? Positive traits? Negative traits?
- When you have conflicts with others, what do you think is causing the problem?
- How would you describe your communication style?

Vignette

Mary H. was relieved when the subject of assessment was introduced. She emphasized that she feels undereducated and out of sync with her peers on the job. Although her computer skills are pretty strong, Mary said she likes customer contact better than sitting at a keyboard all day or teaming with a co-worker.

Mary has received some previous assessment from her community college placement office. She has MBTI scores, a CISS report, and Holland SDS types. You give her the PPS to complete and return at the next meeting.

The CISS matches a client's high skills/interests pairs against a database of good fit occupations. Mary's dominant orientations on the CISS were helping others through teaching, healing, and counseling; and organizing the work of others, managing details, and monitoring results. People with high Helping and Organizing orientations often do well in occupations such as health care administrator, secretary, religious counselor, or patient advocate.

Mary's results on the SDS showed that her three Holland types are: conventional (C: skills in record keeping, organizing data, following through on others' mandates); social (S: working with or helping others); and realistic (R: people who do well in technical, physical, or mechanical activities). Thus, her three-letter Holland code is CSR. The CSR code is related to occupations such as computer operator, operations support specialist, production assistant, quality control specialist, and paralegal.

The MBTI measures natural abilities and preferences. The MBTI manual contains career listings for each of the 16 types. Mary's MBTI type is extroverted, sensing, feeling, and judging (ESFJ). This means she is energized by the external world, she is good with facts and numbers, she makes decisions using her conscience and personal value system, and she likes structured and traditional work environments. ESFJ type is associated with occupations such as receptionist, teacher, nurse, sales clerk, office manager, secretary, teacher, health services aid, librarian, real estate agent, pharmacist, and counselor.

The temperament of an ESFJ person is typically sociable, responsible, thorough, sympathetic, loyal, and cooperative. This person's focus is on facts. He or she is adept at meeting the daily concerns of people by providing practical help and services. An ESFJ person values concrete outcomes and strives for closure in his or her work.

The PPS describes three roles people assume in their daily lives: expected role, default role, and balanced role. The expected role is one's response to present demands, that is, what is asked of us. The default role is behavior from the past that is invoked to handle stress or pressure. The balanced role is a mixture of present and past behavior styles.

Mary's three roles are objective thinker, specialist, and perfectionist. The objective thinker defines, clarifies, obtains information, evaluates, and tests. The specialist contributes a particular area of expertise. The perfectionist maintains an organization's standards and quality controls. All three roles are implementer roles versus leader roles. Objective thinker and perfectionist roles especially suit Mary's technical support capabilities (See Appendix C for publishers of assessment instruments).

Step 4: Interpret the Assessment Data

Whatever the source or amount of data the counselor has been able to gather, he or she and the client must make some sense out of it. What evidence appears time and again? What data are contradictory or inconsistent? Is there a gap in the data picture? Examples of key questions for data interpretation are:

- What new information have we obtained from analyzing your career history and written records?
- What did we learn from the assessment instruments?

Additional key questions for Step 4 include:

- What career matches are indicated by the instruments?
- Are there contradictions in the data?
- How can we explain the contradictions?
- How can we validate our findings?
- How do you feel about the assessment results?
- Do the assessment results clarify why you are having the career issue you described earlier?

In answering these questions, conclusions and themes should begin to appear.

Vignette

Although Mary H. previously participated in some testing, she never analyzed the results in detail. The summary points of the instruments show consistency across the MBTI, the SDS, the CISS, and PPS in terms of occupational indicators. Mary's skills are a good fit for jobs involving data management, helping services, and administrative support. Because her interests are in both data management and customer service, she should concentrate on jobs that are customer-facing, but that allow her to work independently.

Mary likes the role of subject-matter expert. She feels rewarded when providing solutions to meet customer needs. She likes having some distance between herself and others. She prefers working with customers over the phone or via computer. They need and respect her. Although she is a giver, she is not necessarily a sharer. Her security comes from the structure of a stable environment. She likes the job of quality controller, as long as the system is orderly and efficient. Mary is a responder, not an initiator. She works best in the "individual contributor" path.

Step 5: Create a Career Data Profile

In this step, a summary of the data collected is used to highlight key themes that should lead to the solutions to the client's career issues and the career problem. An example of a career data profile form is shown in Appendix D.

Some key questions for use in compiling the career data profile are:

- What are the client's career questions?
- What are the highlights of the job history or career chronology?

- What are the overall themes in the instrument results? What are the career implications?
- What career paths can be eliminated?
- What career paths seem to make sense?

Vignette

Following is a career data profile for Mary H. containing the data presented in this chapter. This document can be used as a reference sheet and focal point for the subsequent stages of the career counseling process: feedback, goal setting, resistance resolution, and follow through.

CAREER DATA PROFILE
Page 1

Name: _____Mary H._____   Dates of Service: _____

Client Career Questions

1. What other jobs am I qualified for?
2. What should I do to prepare for a transfer?
3. How can I leave my present boss/position without creating hard feelings?
4. How do I address my performance issues and create a development plan?

Highlights of Career History

1. Six years: fast food restaurants/customer service/office management
2. Clerical positions: secretary to coordinator, now database coordinator
3. High school diploma—office skills, co-op office experience
4. Two-year degree in office practices
5. Extensive computer training in wordprocessing, spreadsheet, and database software
6. Likes customer interaction
7. Dislikes team interaction, conflict
8. Existing skills: personal computer, data management, product knowledge
9. Skills to develop: proactivity, conflict resolution, time/priority management
10. Positive traits: sociable, responsible, thorough, loyal, cooperative
11. Manager developmental feedback: conflict averse, withdraws from team, reactive versus proactive

CAREER DATA PROFILE		
Page 2		
INSTRUMENT	*RESULTS*	*CAREER IMPLICATIONS*
CISS	Orientations • Helping others through teaching, healing, counseling • Organizing work, managing details, and monitoring results	Some H + O occupations: health care administrator, secretary, religious counselor, patient advocate
SDS	Holland Types (CSR) • Conventional— records/data management, following instructions • Social—working with/helping others • Realistic—technical, physical, or mechanical skills	RIASEC Code = CSR Some CSR occupations: computer operator, operations support specialist, production assistant, quality control specialist, paralegal
MBTI	Type = ESFJ • Extrovert—needs reinforcement • Sensing—likes facts and data • Feeling—conscience and values driven • Judging—conventional and structured	Some ESFJ Occupations: receptionist, office manager, sales clerk, real estate agent, teacher, nurse, librarian, pharmacist, counselor
PPS	Patterns • Expected role—objective thinker • Default role—specialist • Balanced role—perfectionist	Job roles: meticulous about data collection and documentation, subject matter expert, quality control monitor

CAREER DATA PROFILE	
Page 3	
Findings/Remarks	• Primarily trained in office clerical skills • Work experience mainly computer tasks and customer interaction • Strengths include responsibility and loyalty • Shortcomings include conflict avoidance and problems working in a team environment • Career instrument findings show consistent themes: high detail aptitude and helping customers • The instruments suggest careers or roles as an individual contributor in an appreciative environment

Connections to Client Key Career Questions	•"What other jobs am I qualified for?" —Computer operator —Concentrate on jobs that are customer-facing —Find a structured environment that is orderly and efficient —Be a subject matter expert who provides solutions for customers • There are no direct links to the other client career questions at this point in the career counseling process

Chapter Summary

In the assessment stage of career counseling, career records, interview responses, and possible instrument results are collected, analyzed, and recorded in a career data profile. The purpose of the assessment stage is to document a person's existing capabilities, as well as to identify the skills or experiences needed to address the stated career issue. Once the career database is established, the counselor and the client can proceed to the feedback stage of the career counseling process.

Learning Reinforcement

1. Terms and Definitions
    a. *Assessment Stage*: The assessment stage is the second stage in the career counseling process, during which the counselor obtains a career history, administers an assessment package, interprets data, and compiles a career data profile.
    b. *Career Questions*: Career questions are questions the client wants to have answered as a result of going through the career counseling process.
    c. *Interpretation*: Interpretation is a step in the assessment stage where the counselor and client make sense of the data collected.
    d. *Career Data Profile*: The career data profile is a chart containing a summary of all of the information collected from the client's presenting concerns, career history, and assessment instruments.
2. Review Questions
    a. What are the five steps in the assessment stage?
    b. What is the purpose of the client's career questions?
    c. What kind of data go into a career assessment?

      d. What are some frequently used career assessment instruments and what do they measure?

      e. Is it possible to conduct a career assessment without using tests? If so, how?

      f. What is the purpose of the career data profile?

3. Additional Resources

      a. Hood, A. B., & Johnson, R. W. (1991). *Assessment in counseling: A guide to the use of psychological assessment procedures.* Alexandria, VA: American Association for Counseling and Development.

      b. Yost, E. B., & Corbishley, M. A. (1987). *Career counseling: A psychological approach.* San Francisco: Jossey-Bass.

      c. Zunker, V. G. (1990). *Using assessment results for career development.* Pacific Grove, CA: Brooks/Cole.

Chapter 6

The Feedback Stage

The feedback stage begins once all the assessment data have been collected. Remember that assessment includes any referral information, written records, client interview input, counselor observations, and test results (if used). Many career clients report that they cannot be objective when it comes to career decision making. Other clients have piles of records and test results, but not the expertise to apply the data in their career planning. It is the job of the career counselor to teach the client how to make the best use of the data collected during the assessment stage. To that end, there are four steps in the feedback stage: process interview and assessment findings, validate patterns or cycles, link conclusions to client career questions, and outline capabilities and areas for action.

Key Questions: The Feedback Stage

The overall key questions of the feedback stage are:

- What new insights have you gained from the assessment stage?
- What are your conclusions about the data?
- What next step or steps make the most sense after reviewing your career data profile?

Other key questions that could be asked include:

- What overall themes are beginning to emerge?
- What are your tentative conclusions regarding the data?

Step 1: Process Interview and Assessment Findings

The counselor now knows a great deal about his or her client. The counselor has probably developed an hypothesis about the client's career dilemma. It is crucial that the counselor remain nonjudgmental in debriefing the assessment stage results. The urge to jump to conclusions in reviewing the data should be resisted. At this step in the feedback stage, it is critical for the counselor to focus on what is unique about this particular client's career story. This time should not be used by the counselor to tell stories about his or her own career path or to relate anecdotes about other clients. The counselor needs to work collaboratively with the client to make sense of the data. The counselor should use his or her knowledge of the client's history, occupation, and organization as a context for interpretation.

It should be explained to the client that the assessment stage has resulted in the collection of a lot of information. Only some of that information is of relevance to the current career issues. The feedback stage begins by asking the client several key quesitons that focus on his or her reactions to the assessment data:

- How does all of this information sound to you?
- Is this "you" or someone you don't know?
- If you were the counselor, how would you counsel someone with this profile?

Other key questions that could be asked include:

- You have made significant progress in your chosen career path. You now wish to change careers. Why?
- Your assessment data indicate that your current career path is not a good fit for you. Why have you been successful to date despite this misfit?
- Your management considers you a highly valued employee, yet you are eager to leave the organization. How do you explain this discrepancy?

Vignette

Mary H. arrives for the data feedback meeting. You give her a copy of the career data profile for her reaction. Mary H. sees that she has performed well in certain parts of her previous and current assignments, but when her duties do not allow her to work primarily with customers, she does not feel motivated and does not perform well. Mary really wishes that she did not have to work in a team-oriented environment and deal with the pressures she feels regarding her current assignment priorities.

Step 2: Validate Patterns or Cycles

In this step, the objective is to identify patterns or cycles and get the client to realize that these are recurring themes.

Some key questions to use in helping the client clarify and take ownership of the assessment findings include:

- What do all your jobs/assignments have in common?
- What have been the most rewarding components of each of your jobs?
- What have been the most disappointing components?
- What has every boss told you about your performance?
- What feedback has hurt you the most?

The answers to these key questions should be linked back to the career problem and the client's career questions. By now, the client should be making some connections between past experiences and the current career concern.

Vignette

Mary H. says that one characteristic of each of her jobs is that she has been a critical link between the supplier and the customer. She says that she has been rewarded by the acclaim she has received from customers after she has helped them cut through the "red tape." The most disappointing job activities have been those times when she has felt that she was wasting her time dealing with "trendy/flavor-of-the-month, team-oriented stuff."

Mary's bosses have praised her customer-first orientation and, at the same time, expressed the concern that she was becoming too specialized. They have urged her to develop a wider range of skills and attitudes.

She has been most hurt when she has been told that her co-workers don't like her and that they don't want to work with her. She has been told that she is withholding and at times short-tempered. It has been stated that she is "brisk with others." She has also been told that she does not accept negative feedback very well.

Step 3: Link Conclusions to Client Career Questions

In this step, the counselor helps the client use the findings from the assessment stage to address the career problem and client's career questions. Key questions to ask during this step include:

- What are the main messages about the change(s) you need to make?
- What are your preliminary answers to the career problem and your career questions?
- How have you solved other life problems?

Vignette

Mary H. is beginning to realize that she respects her customers more than her co-workers and her employer. In her eyes, customers have all the power. The employer is necessary to "generate her check." She prefers giving most of her time and energy to appreciative customers and very little to her critical co-workers and employer. Mary agrees that before her attitude becomes a total liability she should begin to formulate answers to her career questions.

Step 4: Outline Capabilities and Areas for Action

This is the final step in the feedback stage. The objective is to create a list of actions that will meet the needs of both the client and the employer/organization.

Key questions that need to be answered during this step include:

- What are your strongest capabilities?
- What are your critical areas for development?
- Have you tentatively answered your career questions? What are the answers?
- What do you need to do?
- How do you plan to do it?

Vignette

Mary H. lists her strongest capabilities as computer data management skills, finding quick solutions to customer problems, anticipating future customer needs, and working well on her own.

She identifies several development needs, such as increasing her computer skills and widening her product knowledge. Also, she identifies dealing with conflict and becoming more of a "team player" as skills she probably cannot avoid forever.

As a result of analyzing the data with her counselor, Mary begins to formulate answers to her career questions. She is able to identify some capabilities and areas for action:

- What other jobs am I qualified for in my current department?
  - None

- Should I move to the customer side as a "user"?
  - This might make sense—as a systems utilization specialist

- Should I stay where I am and try to be a sole-source provider to one customer?
  - Maybe—as a technical specialist

- Would it make more sense for me to become an independent contractor and sell services as a technical expert?
  - Maybe—as a systems consultant

- Are there any jobs where I can work on my own and be judged solely on meeting customer requirements?
  - Yes, I think so—customer service representative, technical sales support rep, or technical field rep

- What should I do to prepare for a transfer?
  - I need to meet with my boss and explain to her what jobs I have identified as alternatives to my current position. I would ask for her support in trying to transfer to one of these jobs. I would then prepare a resume that highlights my capabilities to do these targeted jobs. Next, I would identify where these jobs exist and I would prepare a list of people to talk to about my conclusions. Finally, I would develop plans regarding how to apply for these jobs.

- How can I leave my present boss/position without creating hard feelings?
  - I would figure out how it would be in the company's best interest for me to work in another position. Then, I

- How do I address my performance issues and create a development plan?

would have a discussion with
my boss.

- I don't. My boss is right.
  What I'm being asked to do
  is not me. I don't have the interpersonal skills, interest, or
  motivation to address the
  identified development areas. Let's face the truth. I
  don't want to undergo performance reviews that address weaknesses that I am
  either unable to improve or
  unwilling to address.

It is clear to Mary that she has enough strengths and skills to succeed in a
customer-facing job, but not in her current position.

Chapter Summary

In the feedback stage of career counseling, the assessment stage results are
analyzed and conclusions are reached regarding the client's career questions. The purpose of the feedback stage is to identify overall themes, isolate
possible action steps, get ownership/buy-in from the client, and begin
formulating the answers to the client's career questions. Once these actions
have been accomplished, the counselor and the client can proceed to the
goal-setting stage of the career counseling process.

Learning Reinforcement

1. Terms and Definitions
   a. *Career Patterns and Cycles*: Career patterns and cycles are the
      recurrence of rewarding or disappointing components of jobs,
      positive or negative job performance feedback, and similar job
      responsibilities.
   b. *Areas for Action*: Areas for action are decisions that will meet both
      the client's needs and the employer's needs.

2. Review Questions
   a. What are the four steps in the feedback stage of the career counseling process model?
   b. Why is it important to be nonjudgmental in debriefing the outputs from the assessment stage?
   c. What is done with patterns and cycles in the feedback stage?
   d. How does the counselor help the client link conclusions to the client's career questions?
   e. What is the purpose of the outline capabilities and areas for action step in the feedback stage?
3. Additional Resources
   a. Lippitt G., & Lippitt R. (1978). *The consulting process in action.* LaJolla, CA: University Associates.
   b. Otte, F., & Hutcheson, P. (1992). *Helping employees manage careers.* Englewood Cliffs, NJ: Prentice-Hall.
   c. Zunker, V. (1990). *Using assessment results for career development.* Pacific Grove, CA: Brooks/Cole.

Chapter 7

The Goal-Setting Stage

Having debriefed all the available feedback with the client during the assessment stage, the counselor and the client will next be looking for at least some broad indications of choices, directions, or anticipated changes in the client's career focus. In the goal-setting stage, the tasks are to outline the career options, establish priorities, draft preliminary career goals, create a strategic career action plan, and test client and system realities so the client can commit to implementing a plan.

It is important to establish preliminary options and plans at this stage because a client's situation often changes rapidly during the course of career counseling. If a personal crisis or impending job loss is the catalyst for career counseling, the first identified option and plan may not resemble the final course of action because many variables may change before the counseling is completed.

Key Questions: The Goal-Setting Stage

The overall key questions for this stage are:

- In light of everything you have learned, what do you think you ought to do?
- What are the chances of your ideas succeeding, and why?

Step 1: Outline Career Options

Although many ideas may have occurred to the counselor and the client about possible career steps, some organization must take place in order to prepare for decision making. During the exploration of alternatives, the counselor and the client should compile a list or draw a diagram of options to use as a reference during the goal-setting stage. This document can later be used in exercises establishing the client's preferences and the probabilities of success for each option. The counselor can start Step 1 by asking the following key question:

- After our discussions of your job history and the assessment findings, what do you think your career options are?

Key questions that may expand the possibilities are:

- Are there any other options that come to mind?
- Are there any options you have not listed because they do not seem to make sense or because they did not work in the past?
- Do you have the option of doing nothing?

Vignette

During the feedback stage, Mary H. came to the tentative conclusion that she does not want to work on her identified developmental areas. Instead, she wants to seek a position somewhere else in the organization that is customer focused and where she will be able to do her work independently from a team of co-workers. She next identified several other options: (a) leave the organization and find employment elsewhere, (b) leave the organization and go back to school, and (c) leave the organization and become an independent contractor.

Mary was asked whether she sees any other alternatives. Her responses indicated that no other options seemed appropriate to her. After further prompting, she says that she would not consider working for any of her past employers, relocating, or doing nothing about the situation.

Step 2: Establish Priorities

During Step 2 in the goal-setting process, the counselor asks the client to rank the options in order of highest desirability, or highest probability of success. This step is the preparation for writing an actual plan of action. The overall key question for this step is:

- From the list of options, what is the rank order according to the highest probability of success (or rank order according to desirability, simplicity, risk, payoff, or potential for career advancement)?

Many clients have difficulty ranking their options because it signifies commitment to action. Some people resist giving information or answers at this point in the career counseling process because of anxieties about change or unsuccessful experiences with planning in the past. Some clients consider all of their options to be equal. They like to keep all the balls in the air at the same time.

The following techniques can be used to help a client see the value of ranking career options:

1. The client could be shown how to make a fish bone diagram of career options before ranking them. The fish bone contains a center "reference" line, and then a branch for each option, with sublines to the branches containing more detail. Fish bone diagrams often fill up a whole page, creating a visual of how many choices the client actually has. After creating the diagram, it often becomes easier for clients to rank or prioritize the choices. The center line should be used to represent time, risk, payoff, or some other measure. Once the meaning of the center line is identified as a high value for the client, the client can force rank the options in support of that value.
2. The client could be asked to visualize how successful options will look and feel.
3. A force field analysis could be created for each option containing the arguments supporting the option, those opposing the option, and ways of reducing or removing the opposition.

Appendix E contains examples of two of the tools mentioned here. Use of all these approaches is not required when working with a reluctant client. A technique should be used that will help the client establish priorities rather than allowing the ranking process to become stalled.

Vignette

Mary H. feels secure with her first option: seek another position in her current organization. Leaving the company and seeking a position elsewhere was ranked as a second, less desirable option because of loss of seniority and benefits. Going back to school or becoming an independent contractor did not offer her much security. She ranked those choices third and fourth.

Step 3: Draft a Preliminary Career Goal

Once the options have been ranked, the client needs to settle on a preliminary career goal. Following are a series of key questions that could be used to help articulate the goal:

- What has emerged as your primary career goal?
- Is the goal compatible with your career assessment findings?
- Is the goal compatible with your organization's needs and business goals?

Two additional key questions are:

- Are there any new knowledge, skills, motivators, or development opportunities that you need to acquire in order to reach this goal?
- If so, how are you going to acquire these assets in the short term?

Having identified the goal and what is needed to attain it, the next step in the goal-setting stage is to prepare a strategic career action plan.

Vignette

Mary reconfirms that her primary career goal is to move to another position in the organization. Her career assessment findings support this goal. She is not sure that her goal is compatible with either the company's business goals or the needs of her boss. She does not see any need for additional skills, knowledge, or experience, but she agrees with the feedback given during her review that she is not a team player and that she handles conflict poorly. Her conclusion is that the new position needs to be one in which she provides service to customers, rather than working within a team where there is high potential for conflict among co-workers.

Step 4: Draft a Strategic Career Action Plan

The client's primary career goal becomes the center of the strategic career action plan. The purpose of the plan is to spell out in detail what actions will be taken to achieve the career goal, what factors both support and oppose the goal, how obstacles to the plan can be overcome, a proposed timetable, and what resources will be needed by the client to reach the goal. Key questions that facilitate the completion of the strategic career action plan are:

- What incremental steps and corresponding timelines will you be using to reach your career goal?
- What measures will you use to assess both progress toward and success in reaching your goal?
- What forces are propelling you toward meeting your goal?
- What obstacles are in the way of reaching your goal?
- How can the obstacles be reduced or eliminated?
- What resources (people, information, tools, etc.) do you need to reach your goal?
- What is the very next action you will take after leaving today's meeting?

Both Step 3 and Step 4 are ways of developing an overall plan of action. Appendix F contains a strategic career action plan form containing all the key questions used in the last two steps.

Vignette

Mary H. developed a detailed list of steps that she needed to take in order to reach her goal. These included:

1. Put goal and strategic career action plan in writing.
2. Discuss plan with her boss and gain her support.
3. Develop an updated resume.
4. Identify where potential jobs exist in the organization.
5. Network with others familiar with internal jobs to learn specific job requirements; determine if any desired jobs are available; find out who is seeking to fill the jobs; and learn the procedures for applying for the jobs.
6. Apply for appropriate positions.
7. Successfully interview/receive offers.
8. Accept a position.

Mary indicated that she needed to think more about her timeline because she knew her boss was expecting a development plan, not a job-change plan. She said she would measure her progress by the number of steps she completes in her plan.

Mary once again emphasized that the propelling forces driving her plan include the fact that she has the skills, knowledge, and experience to do her chosen work and that meeting customer requirements is what gives her the most satisfaction.

On the other hand, she identified her boss' performance review feedback and getting the support of her boss in seeking a new job as potential obstacles to her plan. She did not have clear ideas about how she could overcome the perceptions held by her boss.

In identifying other resources she might need to rely on in reaching her goal, she suggested interview training and network contacts.

Mary agrees to bring her written plan to the next meeting.

Step 5: Gain Client Commitment

The career goal-setting and strategic action planning process may be impeded if the client is not ready to commit to action and take the necessary steps toward change. The role of the counselor is to help affirm the client's readiness for and commitment to implementation. Some key questions to test readiness are:

- What are the problems or weaknesses of the plan we have discussed?
- What are you doing to correct what's wrong?
- When is your plan going to be put into action?

During this step in the process, either a target date for action is set, or a critical analysis and strategy is introduced for addressing barriers to successful implementation.

Vignette

In previous meetings, Mary stated that her boss' expectations about a development plan might deter her from getting support for an internal job search. So far, Mary has agreed to put her plan in writing and to think about what the timeline should be.

In a subsequent meeting with Mary, she brings her written plan of action, but it has no timeline. Mary is stuck. She fears bringing her plan to her boss because she is convinced her boss will not agree to it and may even take retaliatory action.

Chapter Summary

When the goal-setting and strategic action planning process work smoothly, career options are identified, priorities are established, a goal is chosen, and the action plan is developed and implemented. However, as we have seen in the case of Mary H., a client's newly defined career goal may potentially conflict with what the organization expects from that individual. The tremendous wave of downsizing has caused many of these goal conflicts. Without clear career paths or job security, workers feel they have to fend for themselves. They are less loyal to organizations that do not support them, and are somewhat more inclined to follow their own instincts. When a counselor encounters possible dissonance between client needs and organization needs, he or she may want to use a series of "interventions" designed to locate the source of the "disconnect" and to propose ways of resolving the impasse. Chapter 8 describes these interventions in detail.

Learning Reinforcement

1. Terms and Definitions
   a. *Goal-Setting Stage*: The goal-setting stage of the career counseling process is where career options are identified, priorities are established, preliminary career goals are drafted, a strategic career action plan is created, and client commitment to the plan is obtained.
   b. *Fish Bone Diagram*: A fish bone diagram is a drawing of a fish skeleton used to record outcomes of a brainstorming session. There is a center reference line (the backbone) that usually represents time. There are branches (the fish bones) representing each option, and there are subbranches (smaller bones) containing more detail about each branch. This technique is a useful preparation for rank ordering career options (see Appendix E for a fish bone example).
   c. *Force Field Analysis*: A force field analysis is a method for analyzing the arguments for and against a specified option. Usually the supporting and opposing arguments are written side by side in a chart, showing the "force field" that is created when every positive force has a corresponding negative force. One use of a force field analysis is to see which of the opposing forces can be reduced or eliminated. This technique can be used to evaluate career options (see Appendix E for a sample force field analysis chart).
   d. *Strategic Career Action Plan*: A strategic career action plan is a document that spells out in detail what actions will be taken to

achieve a career goal, the factors that support and oppose the goal, steps that can be taken to overcome the opposition, a proposed timetable, and a list of resources that will assist the client in reaching the goal (see Appendix F for a sample strategic career action plan).

2. Review Questions

   a. Why should a list of options be established before reaching a conclusion about a goal/plan of action?
   b. Why might a client resist ranking his or her career options?
   c. What techniques can be used to help a client see the value of ranking career options?
   d. Why should the counselor help a client identify factors both supporting and opposing a goal?
   e What are the consequences when a client does not commit to the implementation of a strategic career action plan?
   f. What are some key questions that could be used to assist the client during the drafting of a strategic career action plan?

3. Additional Resources

   a. Berg, A. (1990). *Career metamorphosis.* Capitola, CA: SEFA Books.
   b. Hagberg, J., & Leider, R. (1988). *The inventurers: Excursions in life and career renewal.* Reading, MA: Addison-Wesley.

Chapter 8

The Resistance Resolution Stage

The goal-setting stage and strategic career action planning step set the stage for implementation. However, there are times when a client is not ready to act because of internal or external forces that suddenly seem larger than the original reason for seeking career counseling. These forces can be referred to as resistance factors. Resistance is a common occurrence in career counseling and the counselor should be alert to its existence. In any helping relationship, resistance should be viewed as a productive tool for problem solving, not as a barrier to be ignored or pushed aside.

If a client has any signs of resistance, this stage of the career counseling process must be used before proceeding further in the counseling. Ignoring the resistance may cause a failure in the client's implementation of the action plan.

This stage is used to identify the conflicts, assess the sources, resolve the blockages, and link the client to appropriate resources so that follow through can take place.

Appendix G contains a decision tree model that depicts the various paths that, depending on the specific circumstances, should be taken to implement this stage of the career counseling process.

The first decision in the model is to determine if there is resistance. If there is no resistance, the counselor and client should move straight to the follow-through stage. If resistance is identified, the next choice appears:

- Determine whether the resistance is due mostly to internal client variables or mostly to external environmental variables, or some of each.
- If the resistance is due mostly to internal client variables, is it due mostly to a client's internal conflict about change or is it due mostly

to a lack of client capabilities?
- If the resistance is due mostly to internal conflict about change, the counselor needs to implement change tools.
- If the resistance is due mostly to a lack of client capabilities, the counselor needs to use tools to identify missing capabilities.

On the other side of the decision tree, if the resistance is due mostly to external environmental variables, does the resistance center mostly around factors in the work environment or mostly around the counseling relationship/process, or some of each?

- If the resistance is due mostly to the work environment, then the counselor should use tools to assess the impact of the work environment.
- If the resistance is due mostly to the counseling relationship or process, then the counselor and client should revisit the ground rules and the stages and steps in the career counseling process model.

The paths in the decision tree model reveal the types of interventions to employ to reduce or eliminate client resistance.

In complex cases, resistance to plan implementation may be coming from all four sources, so a series of interventions will have to take place before successful completion of the career counseling process can occur. Although multiple interventions may postpone completion of the process, not addressing them will surely result in a return to Stage 1 and a need to review the original purpose of the career counseling. If the resistances cannot be overcome, it is better to start over with a simpler objective than to have the career counseling process fail.

Key Question: The Resistance Resolution Stage

The overall key question for the resistance resolution stage is:

- What conflicts must be resolved in order for you to move forward to implement your plan of action?

Step 1: Identify Conflicts or Impasses to Implementation of the Strategic Career Action Plan

Client awareness and acknowledgment is critical in Step 1 because clients often do not recognize the various forms of resistance. Without this recognition, the client cannot move forward. A counselor can help a client by focusing on his or her complaints or delaying behaviors as forms of resistance. A counselor can help clients understand that, because they have the power to resist, they also have the power to affect the outcome. As a matter of fact, they are the only ones who can resolve the resistance.

This step requires a patient, nonjudgmental, resourceful style of questioning. In addition to the overall key question, a counselor can start this step by asking the following key questions:

- Are you aware of any resistance to acting on your plan of action?
- Who do you think is controlling the outcome of your action plan?

Vignette

Based on the position that Mary H. took at the end of the goal-setting stage, it was necessary to implement the resistance resolution stage. Mary's delaying behavior is reflected by her failure to schedule a meeting with her boss. Mary imagines that she will be punished for coming back with a plan other than the one that addresses her development needs. Therefore, she does not know how to move forward to implement her plan.

Mary tells her counselor that she thinks it is unfair to call her reluctance to meet with her boss "resistance." She says that she is just facing reality. She says that the only sensible thing to do is to put aside her action plan and instead create a development plan that is responsive to the performance review she had with her boss. Mary goes so far as to say that the counselor should not have let her deviate from the original purpose of the counseling.

After further discussion, Mary agrees to analyze the resistance when she is told by her counselor that addressing the resistance will teach her the problem-solving skills she needs to break the impasse.

Step 2: Assess the Source of Resistance

Having concluded that there is resistance to implementing the action plan, the next step is to identify the source of this resistance. In this model, there are four possible sources of resistance:

1. The client has internal conflicts about change.
2. The client lacks certain capabilities.
3. There are blocking factor(s) in the work environment.
4. There is a problem in the counseling process/relationship.

The first possible source of resistance may come from a client's internal conflict about change. This is a common form of resistance. Many people fear the unknown and change, by its very nature, has aspects of the unknown. The resolution of career issues typically requires people to make a significant change. To determine if aversion to change is a source of resistance, the following key questions can be asked:

- Generally, do you see change as good or bad?
- Relative to your action plan, on a scale of 1 (*low aversion*) to 10 (*high aversion*), how would you rate your aversion to change?
- Is change often difficult for you, or is this issue a special case?
- When have you eagerly sought change and when have you been reluctant to change? What were the reasons for the eagerness or the reluctance?

A second possible source of resistance is a lack of client capabilities. Over time, people develop the skills, knowledge, attitudes, and values to perform the duties of a specific job. They also need career management skills, which many clients see themselves as lacking. To determine whether the lack of certain capabilities is the source of resistance, the following key questions can be asked:

- What skills, knowledge, motivators, and development opportunities do you need in order to implement your plan of action?
- How would you describe your career management skills?
- What one or two capabilities are you most motivated to acquire in order to implement your plan?

A third source of resistance may be one or more blocking factors in the work environment. Typical blocking factors include:

1. A highly structured, controlling work environment.
2. A work environment with very limited opportunities.

3. A work environment where risk-taking is not rewarded.
4. A work environment with a large pool of highly qualified job holders.

Uncovering possible work resistance factors could be prompted by using the following key questions:

- How is your work environment structured?
- Is it a high control or low control environment?
- Are there many job opportunities in your work environment?
- Is risk-taking rewarded in your work environment?
- How would you describe your competition for future job opportunities?

A fourth possible resistance factor may be problems in the counseling process or in the counseling relationship. An example is an action plan being crafted or written by the counselor with little or no input or ownership by the client. Another example is the controlling client who does not allow the counselor to go through the stages and steps of the career counseling process. Sometimes the client is holding back, possibly due to trust issues or certain self-defeating behaviors. Uncovering possible counseling-related resistance factors may be prompted by these key questions:

- Where has the counseling process broken down?
- Is it difficult for you to use the career counseling process model?
- Is it difficult for you to work with me and, if so, why?
- At what point in the counseling did you reach these conclusions?
- Why did you feel that you could not express this problem to me before now?

Although the four types of resistance are analyzed separately, the counselor should not be surprised if two or more forms of resistance are found.

Once the sources of resistance are identified, the counselor needs to help the client take ownership of and agree to work at resolving the causes of the resistance. Some key questions in getting the client to own and resolve resistances are:

- Do you think we have accurately identified the sources of resistance?
- Is there a change issue?

- Are there missing capabilities?
- Are there work environment factors?
- Are there problems with the counseling relationship or process?
- Is there a combination of sources?
- Do you recognize certain resistance patterns?

Vignette

Mary H.'s counselor has engaged Mary's efforts to identify the source or sources of resistance to implementing her action plan. Mary reveals that she generally views change as bad because she believes that you almost always lose more than you gain. She rates her aversion to change as a 9 (*very strong aversion*) and says that this situation is highly reflective of how she has dealt with change in the past.

Mary is particularly concerned because she will have to confront her boss about what she really wants to do about her job situation. Mary has already admitted that she is very poor at dealing with conflict and this situation requires a high level of conflict management skill. She is afraid that she will end up with no job at all despite her efforts.

Mary discusses her work environment, explaining that when employees are given a list of development needs during the performance review process, they are required to resolve those deficiencies satisfactorily before management will support any job change.

Finally, Mary lashes out at her counselor, accusing him of encouraging her to develop a career plan that simply would not work. She says that she never thought it was a good idea, but was afraid to tell him because he seemed to think the plan was such a good idea. "If you think its such a good plan, you go and talk to my boss about it."

After considerable discussion with her counselor, Mary recognizes a chance to break out of a pattern of helplessness. The following areas of resistance have been identified:

- Mary's aversion to change.

- Mary's lack of certain interpersonal skills (dealing with conflict and assertiveness).

- Certain perceived consequences in her work environment.

- Viewing her counselor as a negative authority figure.

Step 3: Resolve Resistance Using Tools and Interventions

Once the client has acknowledged the resistance and has agreed to try new behaviors, the counselor can then use the appropriate tools and interventions for each of the sources of resistance. To make sure that the client understands how resolution occurs, the counselor might use some of the following key questions:

- Can you restate the analysis of the resistance in your own words?
- Would you like to try some new behaviors?
- Would you be interested in hearing about and possibly trying techniques that others have used when they found themselves in a situation like yours?

Vignette

Mary H. and her counselor uncover all four categories of resistance. They then proceed to deal with them one at a time, beginning with "internal conflict about change." Mary identifies three change issues:

1. A long history of poor outcomes.
2. A view of herself as "risk-averse."
3. Acknowledgment of problems with authority figures.

The counselor then begins to work with Mary, choosing several interventions to help her deal with the change issues:

- Reduce the emotional component by looking at career decisions as business decisions.
- Identify examples of good business decisions made by Mary in previous change situations.
- Use techniques such as catastrophizing and chunking (see Appendix H).

In support of these interventions, the counselor used the following tools to teach Mary about the nature of change and that her fears were normal and common. The tools give a client a rational, cognitive approach to change (see Appendix I).

- Emotional roller coaster.
- Periods of transition in job change.
- Stages of change model.
- Cost pay-off matrix.

Mary responded quite favorably to these interventions and tools. She eventually concluded that it was time for her to assert herself or lose all that she had worked for. Mary realized that she had outgrown her need for authority figures to make decisions for her and she concluded that the advantages of seeking a job change far outweighed the potential disadvantages.

The second area of resistance focused on Mary's capabilities. She identified poor conflict management skills and poor assertiveness skills as her greatest weaknesses. The counselor then used events in the counseling sessions to counter Mary's negative thinking. The counselor pointed out that during the resistance discussion, Mary had become quite assertive and had not backed off from conflict with the counselor, an authority figure. Other interventions that Mary's counselor used were:

- Reviewing assessment exercises focusing on strengths.
- Reviewing positive performance feedback.
- Analyzing how strengths compensate for weaknesses.

Mary was quite surprised by the balance between her strengths and weaknesses. She concluded that, with a lot of preparation and role-playing, she could handle a discussion with her boss about her original strategic career action plan.

Some additional tools that Mary's counselor could have used in addressing capabilities are listed here and are described in Appendix J:

- Strengths and personal descriptors.
- Managing self/others.
- CCIO model (Challenge, Circumstances, Interventions and Outcomes model).
- Analysis of job.

The third area of resistance was factors in the work environment. With her counselor's help, Mary identified some "givens" that apply to all job seekers in her work environment:

1. A team-matrixed environment requiring strong conflict management skills.
2. A focus on correcting development needs versus changing positions.
3. A general discouragement of job change unless management-initiated.
4. A bias toward employees who are proactive and competitive.

Once the environmental variables were identified, Mary and her counselor devised the following interventions:

- Test the expectations of the various parties to the career counseling.
- Consider re-contracting with the various parties regarding outcome expectations.
- Find people who are supportive of the desired strategic career action plan.

At first, Mary was suspicious about the idea that there might be support somewhere for her plan. As a small step, Mary agreed to discuss her plan with a trusted co-worker. To help Mary reinforce the credibility of her career plan, the counselor used two tools that help explain how factors in the organizational environment sometimes drive the need for job change:

The first tool, "Triggers That Disrupt a Career Routine" is a flowchart that shows the source and number of triggers that can block a person's career path. Arrows in the diagram show what actions can be taken to reduce the blockers, versus what will happen if no change occurs. The second tool, "Linking Individual Needs With Organizational Needs" is a chart that tracks how well an individual is developing the skills that will help the organization meet its business goals. These affirming tools are shown in Appendix K.

These tools finally gave Mary the reality check she needed. She decided that it was not necessary to have a conversation with a co-worker as a preliminary step. The tools had given her the reinforcement she needed to go directly to her boss with her strategic career action plan.

One final source of resistance remained to be addressed—the counselor–client relationship. Mary had stated that the action plan was originated by the counselor and not by her. She had blamed the counselor for creating the plan that had gotten her stuck. To counter this resistance, the counselor retraced the steps from which the plan of action was developed and revisited the roles and responsibilities that had been agreed on with Mary at the beginning of the counseling.

Mary continued to place blame on the counselor until the counselor insisted that Mary review previously used tools (career counseling process handout, Appendix B; career data profile, Appendix D; and the fish bone diagram, Appendix E).

Faced with the cumulative data again, Mary finally realized that it was her own input and accomplishments that led to her action plan.

Step 4: Link Client to Appropriate Resources for Implementation

Once the counselor and the client have resolved all identified resistances by using appropriate tools and interventions, the next step is to link the client to appropriate resources so that the action plan can be implemented. There are many categories of resources that could support plan implementation. These include:

- People resources: co-workers, bosses, mentors, similar jobholders, family and friends, counselors/consultants, and human resource personnel.
- Information resources: printed material, internet sites, video, CD ROM/cassettes, and support networks.
- Financial resources: training and development budget, company benefits, and scholarships/internships/assistantships.
- Experiential resources: volunteer roles, taskforce member, quality work team member, project leader, and rotational assignments.

In order to help the client identify appropriate resources to support the implementation of a strategic career action plan, the counselor could use some of the following key questions:

- What kinds of people could help you ensure successful implementation of your plan?
- Can you name some people you can use as resources?
- What information do you need to obtain in order to carry out your action plan?
- Where do you think you can get this information?
- What financial support do you believe you will need to complete your plan?
- Where might you get this support?
- How might you develop the skills, knowledge, and experience necessary to achieve the desired results?
- Which developmental experiences will bring you the most needed capabilities in the shortest period of time?

Vignette

Having concluded that she should implement her strategic career action plan, Mary H. identified a number of resources that would help her achieve success. These resources included her boss, human resources personnel, internal customers, internal job postings and job bank, company internet home page, women's networking group, funding for internal career center interviewing workshop, and a customer satisfaction quality work team.

Mary believed that she would have a high probability of success if she mobilized these resources and continued to hold herself accountable for implementing her plan of action. She asked her counselor what her next steps should be.

Chapter Summary

In the resistance resolution stage of the career counseling process, conflicts or impasses to resolution are identified, the sources of resistance are assessed, and the resistance is resolved using various interventions. Once this has been accomplished, the goal-setting stage should be revisited to determine whether or not the career goal and the action plan need to be revised. Then appropriate resources for implementation are identified. The client and counselor can then proceed to the follow-through stage of the career counseling process.

Learning Reinforcement

1. Terms and Definitions
   a. *Resistance*: Resistance is the client's inability to implement an action plan because of internal (client-based) or external (environment-based) forces that override the original purpose for seeking career counseling.
   b. *Internal Resistance Variables*: Internal variables are forms of resistance coming from inside the client, such as the client fighting change, or the lack of certain client capabilities.
   c. *External Resistance Variables*: External variables are forms of resistance coming from outside the client, such as factors within the work environment; within the counselor–client relationship; or within the career counseling process itself.
   d. *Implementation Resources*: Implementation resources are specific individuals, information, financial conditions, or experiences that could support the implementation of a client's strategic career action plan.
2. Review Questions
   a. If resistance exists, why must it be acknowledged before proceeding in the counseling process?
   b. How can resistance be used as a productive tool for problem solving?

      c. How does a counselor identify the sources of resistance?

      d. What are some solutions for resistance that stem from obstacles in the work environment?

      e. What are some tools a counselor can use to resolve resistance?

3. Additional Resources

      a. Cotham, J. (1988). *Career shock.* Brentwood, TN: JM Productions.

      b. Freudenberger, H. (1981). *Burn-out: The high cost of high achievement.* New York: Bantam Books.

      c. Gale, B., & Gale, L. (1989). *Stay or leave: A complete system for deciding whether to remain at your job or pack your traveling bag.* New York: Harper & Row.

      d. Jaffe, B. (1991). *Altered ambitions: What's next in your life.* New York: Donald I. Fine.

      e. Sills, J. (1993). *Excess baggage: Getting out of your own way.* New York: Viking Press.

      f. Viscott, D. (1985). *Taking care of business: A psychiatrist's guide for true career success.* New York: Pocket Books.

Chapter 9

The Follow-Through Stage

Having completed the goal-setting stage and, if necessary, the resistance resolution stage, the counselor and client need to ensure implementation of the strategic career action plan and bring closure to the career counseling sessions. Plan implementation and closure are facilitated by applying the five steps of the follow-through stage: transfer responsibility to the client; monitor progress in the implementation of the strategic career action plan; acknowledge closure of the counseling relationship and the formal counseling program; evaluate the effectiveness of the career counseling; and design additional interventions, if necessary.

Key Questions: The Follow-Through Stage

The overall key questions for this stage are:

- Are you ready to manage the implementation of your plan of action?
- How are you going to maintain momentum during implementation?
- How will you monitor your progress in implementing the plan?
- What was the overall effectiveness of the career counseling you have received, and why?

Step 1: Transfer Responsibility to the Client

After a formal program of career counseling, it is essential that the client assume responsibility for carrying out the action plan. In most cases, the counselor will not play any further role, unless future intervention is requested. The agreement is that from this point on, the client is prepared to carry the ball. A key question that could be asked at this step is:

- Is it clear that my role as a counselor has come to an end and that the rest is up to you?

Vignette

Mary H. says that she understands that the formal counseling process has come to an end and that it is up to her to achieve her career objective. She thanks the counselor for the help and insights she has received, and says she feels confident that she can succeed with her plan.

Step 2: Monitor Progress in the Implementation of the Strategic Career Action Plan

In this step, the client looks for ways to assess progress in implementing the plan. Specific events are identified that coincide with the timeline written into the strategic plan. Examples of events that could serve as "checkpoints" for progress are as follows:

- Job ending, business closing, position being eliminated, termination date, etc.
- Performance review dates.
- Internal job posting cycle.
- Completion of project or job rotation assignment.
- Schedule of training courses.
- Company downsizing, merger, acquisition, etc.
- Change in spouse's job.
- Change in present staff.
- Completion of degree program or other training.

Some key questions to help a client monitor progress of the strategic career action plan are:

- What critical events will most likely occur during the implementation of your plan?
- How can you use these events to measure progress in achieving your plan?

Vignette

Mary H.'s action plan included explaining to her boss that finding a customer-facing position such as technical sales support representative or technical field representative would be a win–win solution, especially if the position enables Mary to utilize her strongest skill sets and serve the company's interests. Because Mary originally had been asked to construct a development plan before her next performance review, events most likely to affect her plan progress are:

- The date of her next performance review.
- Availability of jobs via internal postings.
- Availability of appropriate resource people for networking.
- Changes in staffing within her department.
- Completion of projects with current customers.
- Agreement on the part of Mary's boss to support her in her job search.

Because her next performance review is in 3 months, Mary must have her discussion with her boss immediately. Knowing that jobs are posted weekly and that it takes 3 to 6 weeks to complete the interviewing cycle, Mary must start networking and applying for positions immediately. Her current major project will be completed at the end of the month. Rather than take on other large projects, Mary will have to work with her boss and human resources regarding reduction of her job responsibilities. These concurrent events can serve as deadlines by which Mary can pace the implementation of her strategic career action plan.

Step 3: Acknowledge Closure of the Counseling Relationship and the Formal Counseling Program

After transferring responsibility and building in progress measures, the client and counselor need to end the formal counseling program. Some key questions that a counselor might use to introduce this step are:

- How do you feel about how we have worked together?
- How do you feel about today being our last meeting?

Vignette

Mary H. indicates that she was not too trusting when the counseling first started. She was not sure whether this was a set-up. As the sessions progressed, Mary saw that she was contributing just as much as the counselor, and that made her feel as if they were a team. Mary realized that focusing on the tasks of career counseling, as well as her timeline, helped her manage the anxiety that in the past had immobilized her. Mary says that she is ready to implement her action plan.

Step 4: Evaluate the Effectiveness of the Career Counseling

Closure in any relationship or process is enhanced when there is an opportunity to evaluate effectiveness. When career counseling comes to an end, both the client and counselor need to know whether the program achieved its goals, whether the client would recommend the program to others, and whether the client would be willing to participate in career counseling at another point in time.

Informal evaluation may be obtained through a last session discussion with the client, as well as feedback from the referring source. Formal evaluation involves the use of questionnaires, inventories, or self-report forms. The client can evaluate the counselor, the program, and his or her own participation. The counselor can evaluate his or her own performance for developmental purposes. The organization can use grouped data from clients to continuously improve the quality of services offered. Some key questions that a counselor can use in Step 4 are:

- What were the most positive and least positive experiences in your career counseling program?
- What activities were most helpful? Least helpful?
- Are there any subject areas that we did not discuss that you wish had been covered?
- Can you think of any way in which you might have held back in the career counseling process, and why?
- Did you think our communication styles meshed pretty well?
- Would you recommend this service to others with confidence?

If possible, this step should be repeated after the client has completed the plan implementation in order to obtain further data regarding the success of the counseling.

Vignette

During the last session with Mary H., she told her counselor that the most positive experiences in the career counseling were the interpretations of the assessment data and the working through of the stages and steps in the career counseling process. Initially, Mary had no idea that she could create her own plan of action rather than work on the developmental areas her boss had identified. Even if it turns out that there is no job for her at her own company, Mary indicated that she felt resolved enough to conduct an external search and move on to a new career opportunity. Mary explained that initially she had seen her counselor as another authority figure, but through the exercises and handouts, she realized that the decisions had to be made by her, not by her counselor. Mary said that at times she was tempted to introduce more facts about her personal life and concerns. Mary wished the counselor could understand how hard it was for her to make decisions. Mary was able to say that she worked on her career problems despite some personal history of failure. She intends to apply the resistance resolution method to some other areas of her life in which she feels stuck. Both Mary and her counselor agreed that using the stages and steps of the career counseling process helped improve her problem-solving abilities by putting a methodical process to work in conjunction with her instinctive, emotional process.

Step 5: Design Additional Interventions, if Necessary

The disengaged client is now responsible for plan implementation, progress checks, and continuing forward without the assistance of a counselor. However, workplace conditions change rapidly, and depending on how an organization or the public at large uses career counseling services, a counselor may be asked to re-enter the counseling relationship to provide additional services for a client. Any number of events may make further career counseling necessary and appropriate. Termination, a company going out of business, spouse transfer, or a personal crisis, are but a few examples of events of which the client may have had no knowledge during the initial counseling. Some of the key questions to ask in the this step are:

- Are your new career concerns an extension of the work we did together or has something completely new occurred?
- Why are you seeking help from me now?
- Do you need an update visit or a whole new program?
- Am I the right person to be helping you now?
- What steps have you already taken on your own behalf?
- How long do you anticipate the need for my services?
- Does someone have to authorize permission or payment for more service?
- Have you reviewed all our previous materials and the action plan?
- What happened with the previously developed strategic career action plan?
- What is your new career question?

After answering these key questions, the counselor and client should be able to determine whether further career counseling is necessary and if further career counseling is not indicated, what other resources would be of help to the client.

If further career counseling is appropriate, it should be determined whether it makes sense to use the entire career counseling process. If more than 2 years have passed and if the client has changed careers or professions, it might make sense to redo most of the model. In most cases, however, when a shorter time period has elapsed and a client is still on the same career track, the counselor and client determine what stage of the career counseling process should be re-entered.

Some guidelines for where to re-enter the career counseling process are listed here:

1. Re-enter at the foundation stage if there is an entirely new career goal. The foundation stage establishes the background and context surrounding the new career goal.
2. Re-enter at the assessment stage in order to identify new career concerns related to the original career goal. The steps in the assessment stage determine if additional data-gathering or testing is needed.
3. It would be rare to re-enter the career counseling process at the feedback stage because it is closely linked to the assessment stage. However, there might be an occasional situation where new data, such as an unexpectedly poor performance review or a major change in job duties, triggers a return visit by the client. A counselor may be asked to help the client interpret and integrate new data. A new career goal and action plan may then be developed.
4. In the majority of cases of counseling re-starts, the goal-setting stage is the re-entry point. Because of rapid changes in the workplace, clients often return with new career options, reprioritized goals, and outdated strategic career action plans. The steps in the goal-setting stage help the client get back on track and develop a revised strategic career action plan.
5. Re-enter at the resistance resolution stage if the client explains that the plan is still current and valid, but he or she has not been able to implement it.
6. The follow-through stage is never a re-entry point but rather the closing stage for any of the others. The follow-through stage comes after an action plan has been created or revised.

Key questions that can be used to determine what re-entry stage is appropriate follow:

- What has caused you to return for additional counseling?
- Would you call your career issue a new and entirely separate concern from your previous problem?
- Can we use the same data from our previous sessions, or do you have new documents?
- Do we need to collect new data?
- How is your new goal different from your original goal?
- What caused you to get stuck in the implementation of your plan?

Vignette

Mary H. succeeded in her goal of finding a job as a technical support representative for six customers, and she loves her position. She has performed so well that her new boss has suggested an expanded territory that will require extensive overnight travel. Although she would love to have the larger customer base, Mary has some concerns about being away from home for extended periods of time. It would be best if she could wait a year until her divorce is final before accepting the larger workload. However, she is afraid that passing up this opportunity will jeopardize her long-term career aspirations, not to mention a solid relationship with her new boss.

Based on this information, the counselor concludes that additional career counseling is appropriate, and that the best place to re-enter the career counseling process is at the goal-setting stage. Using the steps in this stage, Mary and her counselor can develop a strategic career action plan to address the change in Mary's job responsibilities.

Alternatives to Additional Career Counseling

If additional career counseling is not appropriate, referrals can be made by the counselor for other types of assistance. Other types of helping services are cited here:

1. Employee assistance counselors for personal problems.
2. Marriage and family counselors for domestic problems.
3. Psychologists, counselors and social workers for extended depression, grief, anger, and so on.

4. Financial planners for economic or investment concerns.
5. Books and resource libraries for knowledge building.
6. Support groups for self-help, mentoring, networking, and so forth.
7. Training programs for skill building.

Vignette

Mary H. called her counselor 6 months after their final session. At the time of her follow-up call, Mary had been in her new position for 4½ months. She reported that she liked her new job very much, as well as her new boss and co-workers. They had a much deeper understanding of the system capabilities, as well as long-term relationships with the customers. All seemed to be going well with the plan implementation. There was plenty of on-the-job training as well as an opportunity to attend a national technology conference.

When the counselor probed for the reason for the call, Mary explained that her personal life was still frustrating due to the stalling tactics of her husband regarding a divorce. Mary is ready to move on, but her husband is jealous of her new job and friends. At this point, the counselor gently pointed out that personal counseling falls within the domain of the company's employee assistance program (EAP). Mary countered that she felt much more comfortable confiding in someone she already knew. She feared that the EAP staff would leak her personal business to human resources and that they would pass it on to her new boss and co-workers. The counselor made the observation that just as Mary had learned how to use the career counseling process in a safe and confidential environment, she could also manage the EAP counseling in the same way. The reminder of how Mary came to trust the career counselor encouraged her to make the call to the EAP. Thus, for Mary's current request, a visit with the career counselor was not warranted.

Chapter Summary

In the follow-through stage of career counseling, the counselor maps out the ways in which the client can continue the process. The counselor must clearly transfer responsibility for the plan implementation to the client. The counselor and the client need to identify future events that can serve as progress points in implementing the action plan. The counselor and client formally end the career sessions, aided by an evaluation of the effectiveness of the counseling. A number of events could cause the client to recontact the counselor (e.g., the organization encourages follow-up counseling, events in the workplace or the client's personal life trigger contact, or a flaw is found in the plan). The purpose of the follow-through stage is to prepare for all possible contingencies of plan implementation.

Learning Reinforcement

1. Terms and Definitions
    a. *Checkpoints for Progress*: Checkpoints are specific events that coincide with the timeline of the strategic career action plan. These events can be used to monitor the successful implementation of the plan. An example of a checkpoint might be a performance review, a sunset date for a job ending, or a relocation. A client may want to have a number of career decisions made by a given checkpoint.
    b. *Closure*: Closure is the formal ending of the counseling process, verbally acknowledged by counselor and client. The counselor transfers responsibility for measuring progress to the client.
    c. *Career Counseling Effectiveness*: This is the degree to which a client, counselor, and organization believe the goals of counseling were achieved. Counseling effectiveness can be measured by client self-report and by the use of inventories and checklists.
2. Review Questions
    a. Why does the counselor have to overtly transfer responsibility for plan implementation to the client?
    b. How do external events affect the timeline of the action plan?
    c. How can a client monitor his or her own plan progress?
    d. What are some examples of checkpoints for measuring progress?
    e. Why does closure have to be acknowledged?
    f. What are some of the measures of career counseling effectiveness?
    g. Under what conditions might a client recontact the counselor after the program is over?
    h. How does the counselor determine at what stage to re-enter the career counseling process?
    i. Must the counselor always meet with the client after the program is over?

3. Additional Resources
   a. Geldard, D. (1989). *Basic personal counseling.* Springfield, IL: Charles C. Thomas.
   b. Otte, F., & Hutcheson, P. (1992). *Helping employees manage careers.* Englewood Cliffs, NJ: Prentice-Hall.
   c. Powell, C. (1990). *Career planning today.* Dubuque, IA: Kendall/Hunt.

Chapter 10

Effective Career Counseling

This book is intended to teach counselors how to change or further evolve the way they deliver career counseling. Hopefully, counselors can significantly improve the quality and value of their counseling by using the career counseling process model and key questions provided here, either in whole or adapted to their present methods. The use of the key questions is a major device by which the career counseling process is implemented and collaboration is ensured between counselor and client.

Counselors will face issues and challenges in implementing this model. There are often time limits and environmental factors that affect the use of the model. However, our experience as career counselors and trainers in this methodology has taught us that most users of the model report significant improvement in quality and results from using this systematic approach. This chapter presents a review of what has been discussed throughout the book, as well as suggestions for how to experiment with and periodically assess progress in using the career counseling process model and the key questions.

The Main Contributions of This Book

There are a number of interlocking learning devices provided in this volume. They include a step-by-step model for conducting career counseling; key questions to help counselors proceed through the stages and steps of the career counseling process model; the fictitious case of Mary H. woven throughout the chapters, applying each of the stages and steps to her career concerns; various tools and materials that can be used with the model; and resources for further reading.

Applying the Model and the Process

A systematic approach is recommended for trying out the model in the daily work routine. Counselors should examine the career counseling process they currently use. They should ascertain whether it makes sense for them to adopt the career counseling process model and the key questions technique presented here. Counselors should also question whether there is room in their present methods to supplement or replace some of what they do with the model and techniques presented here.

As counselors go through their analyses, these key questions can be used to compare the career counseling process model with their present systems:

- What portions of the new model will I probably utilize?
- How do I pace myself so as not to interrogate the client?
- Which steps will be the easiest to implement?
- How do I monitor the timing of questions?
- What are the more difficult portions that will require experimentation, skill building, etc.?
- How do I select the best or most appropriate key questions to present to the client?
- How do I make sure my client and I are tracking together?
- What is the best way for me to implement a revised process in my current setting?

One approach might be for counselors to go back to a previous case and compare what was done with the stages and steps in the process model flowchart (see chapter 2). What would have been done differently if the model described in this book had been used? Would the outcome have been different? Would the quality of the career counseling provided have been enhanced? Would the needs of the client have been better met? Would the counselor have been more confident in his or her skills and techniques?

Another approach would be for the counselor to pilot a number of the stages and steps, or the whole model, with selected clients. There may be new business or services for which such a systematic approach would help counselors keep track of results and meet accountability needs. A gradual adoption of the model may be the best way in some environments.

What Has to Happen to Begin Using Key Questions to Drive the Career Counseling Process?

In addition to providing counselors with the structured career counseling process model, we have discussed how to use key questions to trigger the stages and steps in the model. If the use of key questions is new to a counselor, he or she will need to integrate the technique in a way that is natural and that enhances the career counseling. Here are some observations and suggestions to make the transition easier:

- It takes time for a model with this many stages, steps, and questions, to feel natural.
- It may feel artificial and rigid at first versus intuitive and fluid.
- Whatever a counselor's natural style, these questions are intended to increase effectiveness, not impede it.
- Counselors may translate the key questions into their own verbal communication style so that the flow of the sessions is maintained.
- Remember that not all of the key questions are used.

There is no need to use the model and key questions as a precise script. That would be stilted and artificial for any counselor. As counselors gradually introduce the process, they will find their own pace and rhythm. Just like learning a new language, start with vocabulary, then short phrases, then longer sentences, and finally, spontaneous communication.

Another way of integrating the model and key questions into the counseling process is to view career counseling as a mutual discovery process, facilitated by the counselor, in concert with the client. Change in style may require a paradigm shift for some practitioners from a *deterministic* style to an *empowering* style (see Table 10.1).

Review current approaches to career counseling to determine how best to implement the model and key questions.

Issues That Might Arise in Using This Model

There are many issues that may arise as counselors begin to use this model. Some of these issues are discussed here.

TABLE 10.1	
Paradigm Shift	
From Deterministic	*To Empowering*
Telling	Asking
Advice-giving	Exploring
Directive	Client-centered
Jumping to conclusions	Creating options
Consultant as expert	Client as owner
Conventional	Creative

Issue 1: How Can There Be So Many Stages and Steps in a Simple Task Like Career Counseling?

The answer is that career counseling is not simple, it is highly complex. What is needed is a model with stages and steps that mirrors the complexity of the task. A complex model is more applicable to highly varied career counseling situations. For example, if a counselor works with clients in crisis or in chronic underachievement, he or she may encounter resistance in a number of forms. The resistance resolution stage (see chapter 8) uses a methodical approach to identify the source or sources of resistance and successfully resolve the blocks. Many trainees have said that the use of this chapter alone greatly improved their effectiveness as career counselors.

Issue 2: What Do I Do If I Have Little Training or Experience and I Find the Model Overwhelming?

Novices, newcomers, group trainers, and volunteer counselors should think about what works when they personally are seeking help. Do they like a little or a lot of input? Do they like a lot of structure or very little? Do they like intense sessions or relaxed and informal meetings? Have they had any career counseling themselves? What was helpful and not so helpful? Answers to these questions will help counselors integrate this model into their own style of working with others. Counseling skills are acquired through learning and practice. Counselors should give themselves plenty of time to try out the model and the key questions, starting with the parts that come most naturally to them. The key questions are given as prompts to get certain information; select only the key questions appropriate to a particular client's needs.

Issue 3: How Easy Will It Be for Me to Begin Using the Model?

If a counselor has had limited training and on-the-job experience, this may be the first linear model he or she has seen for conducting career counseling. It will be useful to learn and apply the stages and steps before bad techniques are acquired. Those with degrees in counseling and significant on-the-job experience will probably be able to begin using the model immediately, because they will recognize where they are in the sequence of stages and steps with a particular client. It will be easy to use the key questions if directive counseling modalities have previously been utilized.

Issue 4: Do I Explain or Show the Model to My Client?

During the foundation stage, the counselor explains the career counseling process and discusses his or her role as well as the role the client will play. Many clients benefit from receiving a copy of the career counseling process handout (Appendix B) if, in fact, that is the full program they will be receiving. The counselor should modify/simplify this handout to fit the actual situation in order to communicate clearly the actual number of stages and steps that will take place. It is not recommended that counselors distribute the career counseling process checklist with all the stages, steps, and key questions (Appendix A). This document can be overwhelming to a client. It is unlikely that all the key questions would ever be used. If the counselor does show this list to a client, the client might want to jump ahead and skip crucial steps necessary for the development and implementation of a strategic career action plan.

Issue 5: What If I Don't Have Time to Go Through All the Stages and Steps?

This is very likely to be the case in a number of career counseling environments. What is important is a disciplined progression through at least the six stages, using the steps within a given stage that will best serve the client. For example, if there are only 4 hours in which a counselor can work with a client, a compressed model, like the one shown in Table 10.2, might be implemented.

TABLE 10.2

Four-Session Career Counseling Process Model

Hour 1	Hour 2	Hour 3	Hour 4
Foundation Stage	**Feedback Stage**	**Goal-Setting Stage**	**Follow-Through Stage**
(20 minutes)	(30 minutes)	(30 minutes)	(60 minutes)
• Determine the precipitating event • Explain the career counseling process	• Validate patterns • Link data to career concerns	• Draft a strategic career action plan	• Prepare client to measure progress • Designate progress points
Assessment Stage	**Goal-Setting Stage**	**Resistance Resolution Stage**	
(40 minutes)	(30 minutes)	(30 minutes)	
• Identify career concerns • Collect/interpret data	• Outline options, priorities, goals • Gain client commitment	• Identify source(s) of conflict • Remove obstacles	

Issue 6: What If My Supervisor Disapproves of Using this Approach to Career Counseling?

Supervisors may be responsible for the way career counseling is conducted in an organization. Some agencies and firms are required to use specific models or materials and counselors are not free to change those policies. When changes are being considered, however, there might be an opportunity to present this model to the organization.

If no such model or requirements are in place, it is best for counselors to have an open discussion with their supervisors or sponsoring organizations about this model before using it. They should explain their interest in the model, as well as its potential benefits not only to the counselor, but to clients and the organization as well. An experimental approach with a few clients may be appropriate. Another approach might be for counselors to start using key questions wherever they fit in to their existing techniques.

Issue 7: What If I Keep Forgetting the Stages and Steps, or the Model Makes Me More Confused?

Counselors should simplify the model while they are learning it. They should practice one stage at a time and use only one or two key questions per stage or step. They should think of themselves as detectives searching for clues to a mystery: What information must be obtained in order for all the pieces to make sense? The natural order of the inquiry process should be allowed to work for both counselor and client.

Issue 8: Are There Any Cautions in Using the Model?

The stages and steps in the career counseling process model are both linear and cumulative; that is, there is a specific order, and each task builds on the one before it. Skipping around in the model can make it extremely confusing for the client to follow. This does not mean that every line must be rigidly followed, but most clients will follow a logical process better than an unplanned one.

Another caution is over assessment. Once pertinent data has been collected, obtaining additional, superfluous material is not a good use of the client's time or the available counseling time. Pertinent data are facts that answer the client's career questions with sufficient detail to reach conclusions and to develop the strategic career action plan. Spending a lot of time gathering documentation may seem reassuring, but it leaves inadequate time to work through the other stages of the model.

A final caution is the failure to address resistance. The resistance resolution stage was created because many counselors have clients who get stuck in the final stretches of career counseling. Clients backslide in implementing their action plans or their job searches. Some clients repeatedly return for service. It is highly unlikely that satisfactory results will be obtained as long as hidden blocks to action are unresolved. Although addressing and resolving resistance is both challenging and frustrating, it is probably the skill set that best distinguishes the expert from the novice career counselor. Resolving resistance is probably the most valuable take-away for the client, too.

Measuring Career Counselor Effectiveness

Career counselors can measure their counseling abilities, techniques, and results by answering the following questions:

1. How well do I establish career counseling relationships?

2. Do I know the career counseling process model well enough to explain it to someone else?

_____

_____

3. Do I know how to collect relevant career counseling data, whether by interview, records, or testing?

_____

_____

4. How skilled am I at interpreting patterns in assessment data and translating them into usable information for the client?

_____

_____

5. When giving feedback to a client, how well do I link assessment conclusions to the client's career questions?

_____

_____

6. How effective am I in helping the client use the feedback linkages to identify specific areas for action?

_____

_____

7. How well do I help the client identify options, establish priorities, clarify goals, and draft a strategic career action plan?

_____

_____

8. How effective am I in gaining client commitment to implementing the strategic career action plan?

_____

_____

9. What skills do I have in detecting, confronting, and resolving a client's resistance to action plan implementation?

_____

_____

10. In what ways do I successfully transfer action plan implementation to the client and ensure continued monitoring of progress over time?

_____

_____

It is suggested that counselors periodically re-answer these self-evaluation questions as a status check and as a reinforcement of their new learning.

The more the career counseling process model and key questions are utilized, the more progress and improvement can be seen in career counseling effectiveness.

Appendix A

Career Counseling Process Model Checklist

THE FOUNDATION STAGE			
OVERALL KEY QUESTIONS			
• What are the expected outcomes?			
• What counseling has occurred before?			
• Do you understand the career counseling process?			
STEPS	**KEY QUESTIONS**	**DATE**	**REMARKS**
1. Understand the Referral	• What are your reasons for seeking career counseling?		
	• Do all parties agree that this is why we are working together?		
	• If there is not total agreement, what do you need to do so that all parties are in agreement?		
	###		
	• What are your expectations?		
	• How did you decide to seek career counseling?		
	• Who else knows that we are meeting? Did they tell you what they want you to accomplish?		
	• How are the fees for the services going to be paid?		
	• Have you ever been involved in career counseling before? If so, what were the outcomes?		
	• Do you have any copies of previous career counseling assessment materials, action plans, etc.?		
	• Do you have a time limitation or deadline for completing the counseling?		
	• When we are finished, what is the final product going to look like?		
2. Determine the Precipitating Event	• Why are you being sent to me now? • Why are you here talking to me? • If I were to ask your boss why we are working together, what would I be told? • Is this a new situation or one that has been going on for some time? ###		

	• Do you view yourself as being in crisis? If so, what is your support system?		
	• Are you receiving (or have you received) any personal counseling from an employee assistance program counselor, private therapist, minister, etc.? If so, does this person know that you are meeting with me for career counseling?		
	• Do you have any sensitivities about your career, job search, career success, etc.? Do you have any concerns about this counseling?		
	• Are there any cultural issues? Anything tied to lifestyle, race, religion, etc.?		
3. Explain the Career Counseling Process	• In the role of career counselor, I am your guide (sounding board/advocate/resource) for the career counseling process. Your role is to explore all your career options and to communicate how the process is progressing to those to whom you are accountable.		
	• Our work is completely confidential, unless you ask me to provide others with specific career information during a three-way consultation.		
	• I do not provide job placement or personnel recommendations unless we agree that I have the authority to play that role and that it is part of our career counseling agenda.		
	• Do you have any questions before we start?		

THE ASSESSMENT STAGE			
OVERALL KEY QUESTIONS			
• What career data do you have readily at hand?			
• What information needs to be collected?			
• What are the significant findings in the career data profile?			
STEPS	**KEY QUESTIONS**	**DATE**	**REMARKS**
1. Identify Client Career Concerns	• What two or three career questions would you like to have answered as a result of the career counseling? # # # • Are there some unknowns regarding your skills, aptitudes, interests, or values? • Have you received positive or negative feedback about your career choice that you don't agree with? • Have you ever thought that you would be happier in a different job/career/work environment? • Have you been repeating some of the same employment mistakes or patterns? • Three months from now, what would you like to see changed in your career? • Are you managing your career or is it managing you?		

2. Obtain a Career History	• Could you provide me with your resume, your most recent job description, and any performance reviews you might have?		
	• What other job records do you have?		
	• For each of your jobs, what were your responsibilities? What did you like best about the job? What did you like least? What were your major accomplishments?		
	• What is your salary history?		
	• What were you trained for in school? In the armed forces? Tell me more.		
	• Have you had any on-the-job training? Tell me about it.		
	• What are your strongest job skills? Your weakest?		
	• Have you ever participated in any multisource feedback process? If so, do you have notes or reports?		
	• Have you participated in any workshops where co-workers were asked to give you feedback on communication style or team behaviors? What feedback did you receive?		
	• What career path have you been following?		
3. Select and Administer Assessment Tools	• Have you ever completed any career or aptitude testing? If so, please bring copies of the scores or reports to our next session.		
	• Have you ever completed instruments for the purpose of clarifying your career goals and making better decisions? If yes, can you bring copies to our next session?		
	# # #		
	• What are your strongest skill sets?		
	• In what skill areas have you shown the most improvement over time?		
	• What job activities do you most enjoy?		
	• How do you spend most of your time on the job?		
	• What skills have you been able to teach others?		
	• What motivates you on the job? What demotivates you on the job?		
	• How do others see you? Positive traits? Negative traits?		
	• When you have conflicts with others, what do you think is causing the problem?		
	• How would you describe your communication style?		
4. Interpret the Assessment Data	• What new information have we obtained from analyzing your career history and written records?		
	• What did we learn from the assessment instruments?		
	# # #		
	• What career matches are indicated by the instruments?		
	• Are there contradictions in the data?		

	• How can we explain the contradictions?		
	• How can we validate our findings?		
	• How do you feel about the assessment results?		
	• Do the assessment results clarify why you are having the career issue you described earlier?		
5. Create a Career Data Profile	• What are the client's career questions? • What are the highlights of the job history or career chronology?		
	• What are the overall themes reflected in the instrument results? What are the career implications?		
	• What career paths can be eliminated? • What career paths seem to make sense?		

THE FEEDBACK STAGE				
OVERALL KEY QUESTIONS				
• What new insights have you gained from the assessment stage?				
• What are your conclusions about the data?				
• What next step or steps make the most sense after reviewing your career data profile?				
Other Key Questions				
• What overall themes are beginning to emerge?				
• What are your tentative conclusions regarding the data?				

STEPS	KEY QUESTIONS	DATE	REMARKS
1. Process Interview and Assessment Findings	• How does all of this information sound to you? • Is this "you" or someone you don't know? • If you were the counselor, how would you counsel someone with this profile? ### # # • You have made significant progress in your chosen career path. You now wish to change careers. Why? • Your assessment data indicate that your current career path is not a good fit for you. Why have you been successful to date despite this misfit? • Your management considers you a highly valued employee, yet you are eager to leave the organization. How do you explain this discrepancy?		
2. Validate Patterns or Cycles	• What do all of your jobs/assignments have in common? • What have been the most rewarding components of each of your jobs? • What have been the most disappointing components? • What has every boss told you about your performance? • What feedback has hurt you the most?		

3. Link Conclusions to Client Career Questions	• What are the main messages about the change(s) you need to make? • What are your preliminary answers to the career problem and your career questions? • How have you solved other life problems?		
4. Outline Capabilities and Areas for Action	• What are your strongest capabilities? • What are your critical areas for development? • Have you tentatively answered your career questions? What are the answers? • What do you need to do? • How do you plan to do it?		

THE GOAL–SETTING STAGE			
OVERALL KEY QUESTIONS			
• In light of everything you've learned, what do you think you ought to do?			
• What do you think are the chances of your ideas succeeding, and why?			
STEPS	**KEY QUESTIONS**	**DATE**	**REMARKS**
1. Outline Career Options	• After our discussions of your job history and the assessment findings, what do you think your career options are? ### # • Are there any other options that come to mind? • Are there any options you have not listed because they do not seem to make sense or because they did not work in the past? • Do you have the option of doing nothing?		
2. Establish Priorities	• From the list of options, what is the rank order according to the highest probability of success (or rank order according to simplicity, risk, payoff, or potential for career advancement)?		
3. Draft a Preliminary Career Goal	• What has emerged as your primary career goal? • Is the goal compatible with your career assessment findings? • Is the goal compatible with your organization's needs and business goals? • Are there any new knowledge, skills, motivators, or development opportunities that you need to acquire in order to reach this goal? • If so, how are you going to acquire these assets in the short term?		
4. Draft a Strategic Career Action Plan	• What incremental steps and corresponding timelines will you be using to reach your career goal? • What measures will you use to assess both progress toward and success in reaching your goal? • What forces are propelling you toward meeting your goal? • What obstacles are in the way of reaching your goal? • How can the obstacles be reduced or eliminated?		

		DATE	REMARKS
	• What resources (people, information, tools, etc.) do you need to reach your goal?		
	• What is the very next action you will take after leaving today's meeting?		
5. Gain Client Commitment	• What are the problems or weaknesses of the plan we have discussed?		
	• What are you doing to correct what's wrong?		
	• When is your plan going to be put into action?		

THE RESISTANCE RESOLUTION STAGE			
OVERALL KEY QUESTION			
• What conflicts must be resolved in order for you to move forward to implement your plan of action?			
STEPS	**KEY QUESTIONS**	**DATE**	**REMARKS**
1. Identify Conflicts or Impasses to the Implementation of the Action Plan	• Are you aware of any resistance to acting on your plan of action? • Who do you think is controlling the outcome of your action plan?		
2. Assess the Source(s) of Resistance	*Internal Conflict About Change* • Generally, do you see change as good or bad? • Relative to your action plan, on a scale of 1 (low aversion) to 10 (high aversion), how would you rate your aversion to change? • Is change often difficult for you, or is this issue a special case? • When have you eagerly sought change and when have you been reluctant to change? What were the reasons for the eagerness or the reluctance? *Client Capabilities* • What skills, knowledge, motivators, and development opportunities do you need in order to implement your plan of action? • How would you describe your career management skills? • What one or two capabilities are you most motivated to acquire in order to implement your plan? *Factors in the Work Environment* • How is your work environment structured? • Is it a high control or low control environment? • Are there many job opportunities in your work environment? • Is risk-taking rewarded in your work environment? • How would you describe your competition for future job opportunities?		

		Counseling Process or Relationship		
		• Where has the counseling process broken down?		
		• Is it difficult for you to use the career counseling process model?		
		• Is it difficult for you to work with me and, if so, why?		
		• At what point in the counseling did you reach these conclusions?		
		• Why did you feel that you could not express this problem to me before now?		
		Owning and Resolving Resistances		
		• Do you think we have accurately identified the sources of resistance?		
		• Is there a change issue? • Are there missing capabilities?		
		• Are there work environment factors?		
		• Are there problems with the counseling relationship or process?		
		• Is there a combination of sources?		
		• Do you recognize certain resistance patterns?		
3. Resolve Resistance Using Tools and Interventions		• Can you restate the analysis of the resistance in your own words? • Would you like to try some new behaviors? • Would you be interested in hearing about and possibly trying techniques that others have used when they found themselves in a situation like yours?		
4. Link Client to Appropriate Resources for Implementation		• What kinds of people could help you ensure successful implementation of your plan? • Can you name some people you can use as resources? • What information do you need to obtain in order to carry out your action plan?		
		• Where do you think you can get this information?		
		• What financial support do you believe you will need to complete your plan?		
		• Where might you get this support?		
		• How might you develop the skills, knowledge, and experience necessary to achieve the desired results?		
		• Which developmental experiences will bring you the most needed capabilities in the shortest period of time?		

THE FOLLOW–THROUGH STAGE			
OVERALL KEY QUESTIONS			
• Are you ready to manage the implementation of your plan of action?			
• How are you going to maintain momentum during implementation?			
• How will you monitor your progress in implementing the plan?			
• What was the overall effectiveness of the career counseling you have received, and why?			
STEPS	**KEY QUESTIONS**	**DATE**	**REMARKS**
1. Transfer Responsibility to the Client	• Is it clear that my role as a counselor has come to an end and that the rest is up to you?		
2. Monitor Progress in the Implementation of the Strategic Career Action Plan	• What critical events will most likely occur during the implementation of your plan? • How can you use these events to measure progress in achieving your plan?		
3. Acknowledge Closure of the Counseling Relationship and the Formal Counseling Program	• How do you feel about how we have worked together? • How do you feel about today being our last meeting?		
4. Evaluate the Effectiveness of the Career Counseling	• What were the most positive and least positive experiences in your career counseling program? • What activities were most helpful? Least helpful? • Are there any subject areas that we did not discuss that you wish had been covered? • Can you think of any way in which you might have held back in the career counseling process, and why? • Did you think our communication styles meshed pretty well? • Would you recommend this service to others with confidence?		
5. Design Additional Interventions, if Necessary	• Are your new career concerns an extension of the work we did together or has something completely new occurred? • Why are you seeking help from me now? • Do you need an update visit or a whole new program? • Am I the right person to be helping you now? • What steps have you already taken on your own behalf? • How long do you anticipate the need for my services? • Does someone have to authorize permission or payment for more service? • Have you reviewed all our previous materials and the action plan? • What happened with the previously developed strategic career action plan?		

	• What is your new career question?		
	Re-Entry Questions		
	• What has caused you to return for additional counseling?		
	• Would you call your career issue a new and entirely separate concern from your previous problem?		
	• Can we use the same data from our previous sessions, or do you have new documents?		
	• Do we need to collect new data?		
	• How is your new goal different from your original goal?		
	• What caused you to get stuck in the implementation of your plan?		

Appendix B

Career Counseling Process Handout

I. The Foundation Stage
    A. Determine how the client was referred for career counseling.
    B. Record client career questions to be answered. Understand why career counseling is presently being sought. Discuss client concerns and expectations and third-party consultation.
    C. Explain the career counseling process.

II. The Assessment Stage
    A. Collect pertinent data via documents, interviews, observation, and feedback from others. Build career history (including critical events). Review resume, job descriptions, performance data, etc.
    B. Administer assessment tools. Develop career data profile.

III. The Feedback Stage
    A. Process assessment and interview findings with the client. Validate patterns or cycles. Connect assessment findings to other significant events in client's career.
    B. Outline capabilities and areas for action. Determine if data answer the client's career questions.

IV. The Goal-Setting Stage
    A. Outline career options. Set priorities.
    B. Draft preliminary career goals, considering data collected and system constraints.
    C. Draft a strategic career action plan and gain commitment to implementation.

V. The Resistance Resolution Stage
   A. Identify impasses to action.
      1. Internal variables within the client.
      2. Skill/performance deficits.
      3. Organizational/system variables.
      4. Counseling process/counseling relationship problem.
   B. Resolve the resistance using tools and interventions.
   C. Link client to appropriate resources for implementation.

VI. The Follow-Through Stage
   A. Transfer responsibility to the client.
   B. Monitor checkpoints in the strategic career action plan.
   C. Provide closure to the counseling process.
   D. Design additional interventions, if necessary.

Appendix C

Career Assessment Materials and Publishers

PUBLISHER	INSTRUMENT NAME	CATEGORY
Consulting Psychologist's Press (CPP) 3808 E. Bayshore Road Palo Alto, CA 94303 1-800-624-1765	• Myers-Briggs Type Indicator (MBTI) • Strong Campbell Interest Inventory (SCII) • Career Development Inventory (CDI; Super et al.)	Personality Career interests Career decision readiness
Psychological Assessment Resources, Inc. (PAR) P.O. Box 998 Odessa, FL 33556 1-800-331-TEST	• Holland's Self-Directed Search (SDS)	Career interests
Ten Speed Press Box 7123 Berkeley, CA 94707 1-800-841-BOOK	• Quick Job Hunting Map	Skills inventory
National Computer Systems (NCS) P.O. Box 1416 Minneapolis, MN 55440 1-800-627-7271	• Campbell Interest and Skills Survey (CISS)	Interests and skills
Carlson Learning Co. P.O. Box 59159 Minneapolis, MN Distributor: Luella Jackson (847) 205-0559	• Personal Profile System (PPS; also known as the DiSC)	Roles and behaviors
University Associates 7596 Eads Avenue LaJolla, CA 92037	• Career Anchors (Schein) • Decision-Style Inventory	Self-perceived talents, abilities, motives, values, and needs Effectiveness of decisions
Personnel Decisions Inc. (PDI) Forshay Tower Suite 2300521 Marquette Avenue Minneapolis, MN 55402 1-800-633-4410	• Management Skills Profile (MSP) • The Profiler®	Eight dimensions of management skills 360° feedback

PUBLISHER	INSTRUMENT NAME	CATEGORY
Human Synergistics 39819 Plymouth Road Plymouth, MI 48170	• Lifestyles • Management Effectiveness Profile System	Values Management skills
Teleometrics, International P.O. Drawer 1850 Conroe, TX 77301	• Work Motivation Inventory (Hall & Williams)	Measures needs based on Maslow's hierarchy
California Test Bureau McGraw-Hill 20 Ryan Ranch Road Monterey, CA 93940 (800) 538-9547	• Career Maturity Inventory (CMI; Crites)	Realism of career choices

Workbooks

Bierman House Bedford, NY	• *If You Knew Who You Were You Could Be Who You Are* by Gerald M. Sturman, PhD, 1992	Self-paced career assessment and planning system
Gorsuch Scarisbrick Publishers, Scottsdale, AZ	• *The Career Fitness Program,* by Sukiennik, Bendat, and Raufman, 1989	Do-it-yourself assessment journal leading to a job search strategy

Computer-Based Systems

ACT 2201 N. Dodge St. P.O. Box 168 Iowa City, IA 52243 (319) 337-1000	• DISCOVER • DISCOVER FOR ORGANIZATIONS	These are computer-based career management systems that allow students or employees to input their interests, skills, values, and preferences to be matched against a database of occupations or job openings
Career Ware - ISM Systems Industrial Park, Building 3 Ogdensburg, NY 13669 (800) 267-1544	• Choices CT	Evaluative system for adults in career transition

Appendix D

Career Data Profile

Page 1

Name:_____Dates of Service:_____

Client Career Questions

1.

2.

3.

4.

5.

Highlights of Career History

1.

2.

3.

4.

5.

Career Data Profile

Page 2

INSTRUMENT	RESULTS	CAREER IMPLICATIONS

Career Data Profile

Page 3

Findings/Remarks
Connection to Client **Key Career Questions**

Appendix E

Clarification Tools: Fish Bone Diagram and Force Field Analysis

Fish Bone Diagram

A fish bone diagram is a drawing of a fish skeleton used to record outcomes of a brainstorming session. The exercise starts by drawing a center reference line (the backbone) that represents time. There are branches (the fish bones) representing each option, and there are sub-branches (smaller bones) containing more detail about each branch. This technique is a useful preparation for rank ordering career options.

Directions: After detailing options on the fish bones, rank order your choices as you see them today (1 = best).

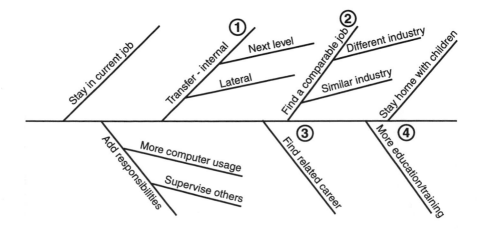

Force Field Analysis

On the left side, list the forces propelling you toward your desired change. On the right side, list the obstacles working against each of the forces for change.

Forces for Change	**Forces Against Change**

Which of the forces against change can be reduced, and in what way?

_____

_____

_____

_____

Appendix F

Strategic Career Action Plan

Name: _____ Date: _____

1. After reviewing the findings from this evaluation process, what is emerging as your primary career or development goal?

   _____
   _____
   _____

2. How is this goal related to the assessment findings?

   _____
   _____
   _____

3. How does this goal fit with your organization's mission and business goals?

   _____
   _____
   _____

4. What new knowledge, skills, motivators, and development opportunities do you need to reach your goal? Complete the chart on next page.

A. Knowledge	**B. Skills**
What new theories, technologies, or approaches do you need to learn to help you reach your goal?	What skills do you need to acquire, update, or use more often to help you reach your goal?
Theories:	Soft Skills:
Technologies:	Management/Administrative Skills:
Approaches:	Technical Skills:
C. Motivators	**D. Development Opportunities**
What kind of reinforcers do you need to perform to your full potential?	What opportunities, such as training, a promotion, a mentor, challenging projects, graduate school, etc., do you need to help you reach your goal?
On-the-Job Reinforcers:	On the Job:
Outside the Workplace:	Outside the Workplace:

5. What incremental steps and corresponding timeline will you use to reach your goal?

Steps				
Timeline				

6. What measures will you use to assess both progress toward and success in reaching your goal?

_____

_____

7. What forces are propelling you toward meeting your goal?

8. What obstacles are in the way of reaching your goal?

9. Which obstacles can be reduced or eliminated and in what way?

10. What resources (people, information, funds, etc.) do you need to reach your goal?

11. What additional help do you need from the consultant?

12. What is the very next goal action you will take after leaving today's meeting?

Appendix G

Resistance Resolution Decision Tree

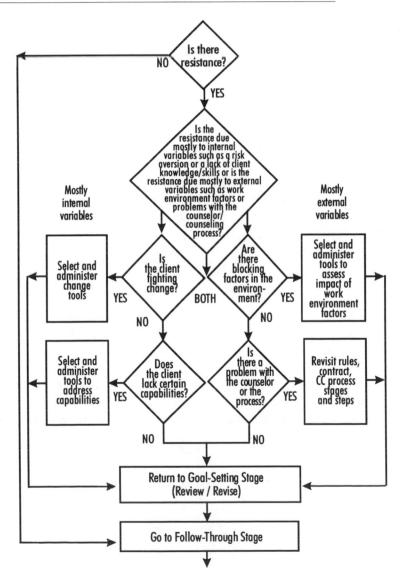

Appendix H

Change Techniques:
Catastrophizing and Chunking

Catastrophizing

Catastrophizing is a verbal or written exercise in which a counselor helps a client confront risk anxiety by verbalizing worst-case scenarios:

- What is the worst thing that can happen with this career decision?
- If the worst does happen, how will you deal with it?
- Who can you get to support you if the worst happens?
- What is your back-up plan?

Chunking

Sometimes a career decision turns out to be too big of a step. Break the decision into chunks, thereby spreading the risk and getting used to change in smaller increments.

- What are some smaller steps you could take to test out the larger decision?
- How does taking smaller steps help to clarify what actions you should take?

Appendix I

Intervention Tools:
Emotional Roller Coaster, Periods of
Transition in Job Change, Stages of
Change Model, and Cost Payoff Matrix

Emotional Roller Coaster

First 2 Weeks   The Next 6-10 Weeks   Until New Job

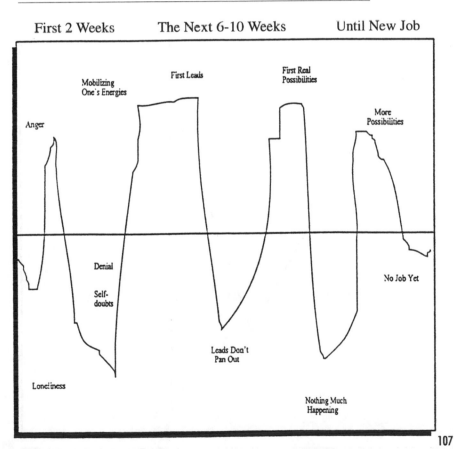

Periods of Transition in Job Change

First Stages	Transition Period	New Beginnings
• Resistance	• Disorganization	• Reorganization
• Loss	• Sadness	• High Energy
• Anger	• Uncertainty	• New Challenges
• Pain	• Fear	• Closure
• Denial		

Stages of Change Model

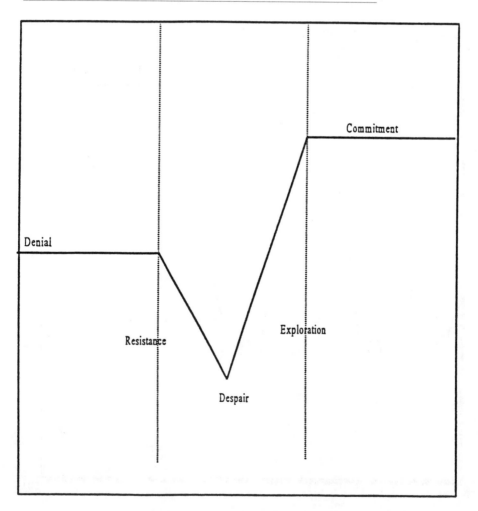

Cost Payoff Matrix

	High Cost	Low Cost
High Payoff	I. Tough decisions. High risk, but often best rewards.	III. Bargain decisions! Big rewards with low investment.
Low Payoff	II. Disappointments. Life's lessons. Analyze carefully.	IV. Easy decisions. Easy experiments. Often precursors to bigger steps.

- In which quadrant do you make most of your career or job decisions?
- Can you make a better decision by moving to another quadrant?

Appendix J

Tools to Address Capabilities: Strengths and Personal Descriptors, Managing Self/Others, CCIO Model, and Analysis of Job

Strengths and Personal Descriptors

Instructions: Read the following list of strengths and personal descriptors. Check (✓) each item you believe applies to you. After checking all applicable items, go back and circle 8 to 12 of your strongest characteristics (those you do well and like to do/best describe you).

___ Able	___ Caring	___ Depressed
___ Able to Memorize	___ Certain	___ Determined
___ Achiever	___ Challenging	___ Dignified
___ Active	___ Cheerful	___ Diplomatic
___ Adaptable	___ Childish	___ Direct
___ Administration	___ Coaching	___ Disciplined
___ Adventurous	___ Counseling	___ Discreet
___ Aggressive	___ Cocky	___ Do Gooder
___ Alert	___ Competent	___ Doer
___ Aloof	___ Competitive	___ Domineering
___ Ambitious	___ Confident	___ Drawing
___ Analytical	___ Conforming	___ Driven
___ Analyze	___ Conscientious	___ Editing
___ Animated	___ Controlled	___ Effervescent
___ Anticipate	___ Controlling	___ Efficient
___ Articulate	___ Cooperative	___ Emotional
___ Artistic	___ Coordinate	___ Energetic
___ Assertive	___ Courteous	___ Enterprising
___ Attractive	___ Creative/New Ideas	___ Enthusiastic
___ Bold	___ Critical	___ Expressive
___ Bright	___ Curious	___ Extroverted
___ Calm	___ Decisive	___ Fair
___ Carefree	___ Dependable	___ Flexible

Strengths and Personal Descriptors (continued)

___ Follow-Through
___ Follower
___ Forceful
___ Free Spirit
___ Friendly
___ Funny
___ Gentle
___ Giving
___ Glib
___ Gregarious
___ Handle Details
___ Hard Worker
___ Honest
___ Honorable
___ Humorous
___ Imaginative
___ Independent
___ Ingenious
___ Innovative
___ Inspiring
___ Introverted
___ Intuitive
___ Inventive
___ Investigating
___ Judgmental
___ Knowledgeable
___ Leader
___ Leading Discussion
___ Listener
___ Lively
___ Logical
___ Loyal
___ Mature
___ Methodical
___ Negotiator
___ Noncommittal

___ Numerical
___ Observant
___ Operate Equipment Well
___ Optimist
___ Oral Communication
___ Organized
___ Organizer
___ Original
___ Outgoing
___ PC Skills (Good)
___ Perceptive
___ Perfectionist
___ Personable
___ Persuasive
___ Pessimist
___ Plan
___ Pleasant
___ Pragmatic
___ Precise
___ Preventative
___ Problem Solver
___ Programming
___ Progressive
___ Punctual
___ Questioning
___ Quick Learner
___ Quiet
___ Rambler
___ Rational
___ Realistic
___ Reasonable
___ Relating/Teamworker
___ Relaxed
___ Reliable
___ Researcher

___ Respectful
___ Responsible
___ Sales Expertise
___ Schedule
___ Secure
___ Self-confident
___ Self-reliant
___ Self-starter
___ Sensitive
___ Serious
___ Sharp Dresser
___ Sincere
___ Sociable
___ Soft Spoken
___ Sophisticated
___ Stable
___ Striver
___ Strong Clerical Skills
___ Supervise Very Well
___ Supportive
___ Systematic
___ Tactful
___ Tenacious
___ Tolerant
___ Tough
___ Training Skills
___ Trusting
___ Trustworthy
___ Wise
___ Work with Tools
___ Writes Well
___ Written Communication
___ Youthful
___ Zestful

Strengths and Personal Descriptors (continued)

Analysis and Application

- Do you notice any patterns? Trends?
- In your past jobs, were you doing what you're good at and what you like to do?
- Can you target your job search to optimize your strengths and what you like to do?
- What are your three major strengths? What are your five key descriptors? Not all of your strengths/personal descriptors will be applicable to all jobs for which you interview. In these instances, how can you optimize one set of strengths/personal descriptors versus another?
- Use this information when developing content for your resume, job interviews, and networking conversations.

Strengths/Personal Descriptors Worksheet

Instructions: Do this exercise after completing the Strengths and
Personal Descriptors exercise. Identify a work-related
situation that demonstrates the effective use of one of
your major strengths or personal descriptors. Write a
detailed narrative explaining the situation, specific actions that you took to deal with the situation and the
results of your actions. Specifically explain how you
contributed to the positive outcome.

Strength/Personal Descriptor: _____

Situation and Actions Taken:

_____
_____
_____
_____
_____

Results: (Describe how you specifically contributed to the positive outcome.)

_____
_____
_____
_____
_____

Application:
This activity will help you identify specific, work-related experiences in
which you have used/showcased your strengths.

Managing Self / Others

This exercise is designed to help you identify your strengths (or deficiencies) in managing yourself and others. It may help you identify the types of job responsibilities for which you are best suited.

Instructions: Assess yourself on each dimension using the rating scale noted below.

Rating Scale: 1 = low
2 = below average
3 = above average
4 = high
N/A = not applicable

RATING

Job Knowledge

1. Demonstrates understanding of principles and theory applicable to task   _____

2. Demonstrates knowledge of issues, problems, and/or innovations specific to industry   _____

3. Expands specialized knowledge and skills required in the job   _____

4. Readily grasps and masters new job requirements   _____

Total Points: _____
Average (divide total points by 4):   _____

Management Capability

1. Meets cost effectiveness, quality control, and performance standards   _____

2. Recognizes and analyzes causes of problems   _____

3. Generates alternatives and solutions to problems   _____

4. Sets realistic goals   _____

5. Effectively organizes work   _____

6. Monitors and follows through   _____

7. Directs and is willingly responsible for performance of others   _____

Total points: _____
Average (divide total points by 7):   _____

Managing Self / Others (continued)

RATING

Action-Taking Ability

1. Takes initiative in finding solutions to problems _____

2. Meets deadlines _____

3. Achieves balance between work quality and quantity _____

4. Takes prompt and proper action within authorized scope _____

5. Makes sound decisions _____

6. Shows personal motivation, builds on strengths and works on deficiencies _____

Total Points: _____
Average (divide total points by 6): _____

Human Relations Skills

1. Evaluates and develops subordinates effectively _____

2. Participates well as part of a team _____

3. Communicates effectively (written) _____

4. Communicates effectively (oral) _____

5. Motivates and influences colleagues and subordinates _____

6. Has leadership ability _____

7. Forms positive relationships with others _____

Total Points: _____
Average (divide total points by 7): _____

Analysis and Application

Do you see more 1's or 2's in any particular dimension? 3's or 4's? What is your strongest area?

Where do you need professional growth?

What are you currently doing or planning to do in order to foster your development?

Before you complete this exercise, make a copy and share it with a work associate whom you know and trust. Ask him/her to complete this exercise and share the responses with you. Do your perceptions match? What perceptual gaps exist?

Use this exercise to help you explore your interest and readiness to work in a particular management position.

CCIO MODEL

CHALLENGE, CIRCUMSTANCES, INTERVENTIONS, AND OUTCOMES

During job search, it is essential to be able to quickly recall and describe how you address challenges on the job. You can use the CCIO Model to prepare and rehearse examples of your problem-solving skills. Create several examples, using different skill sets for use in interviews and on your resume.

There are four parts in the CCIO Model:

1. CHALLENGE Describe a work-related challenge, issue, project, job duty or personal objective.

Example: After three months on the job, I was told I had to cut my budget by 20% within two months.

2. CIRCUMSTANCES Describe the setting, external and internal factors, your role, and barriers to successfully addressing the challenge.

Example: As a new supervisor in the company, I was faced with announcing unfavorable cuts in an already tight budget. Having come from a competitor company, my new direct reports had both positive and negative expectations about my role.

3. INTERVENTIONS List the specific steps that you took (and/or the skills you used) to address the challenge:

Example:
- *Reviewed last three years of department budget records;*
- *Called a team meeting for input on budget priorities;*
- *Used consensus to gain commitment to necessary cuts;*
- *Reestablished priorities for gaining new business to offset cuts.*

4. OUTCOMES State the outcomes that reflect your role/actions in intervening and addressing the challenge. Use numerical dimensions whenever possible.

Example: Reduced expenditures by 24% ($120 K) in required time period, while targeting a 30% increase in new business in the next two quarters.

Analysis of Job

Instructions: Use this form for recording information that you can use in talking or writing about each job that you have held. The Major Accomplishments section should include results in measurable terms such as dollar volume, % increase or decrease in productivity or time, or dimensions of a project or program.

Job Title: _____

_____

Duties/Responsibilities: _____

_____

Major Accomplishments:

1. _____
_____
_____

2. _____
_____
_____

3. _____
_____
_____

4. _____
_____
_____

5. _____
_____
_____

Appendix K

Tools to Affirm the Plan:
Triggers That Disrupt a Career Routine
and Linking Individual Needs With
Organizational Needs

Triggers That Disrupt a Career Routine

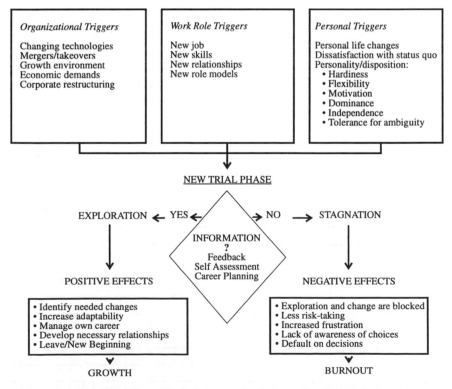

Adapted from "Career Development Theory in Organizations," Chapter 13, p. 434, Douglas T. Hall, in *Career Choice and Development*. Brown, D., Brooks, L., and Associates (Eds.) (1990). San Francisco: Jossey-Bass.

Linking Individual Needs With Organizational Needs

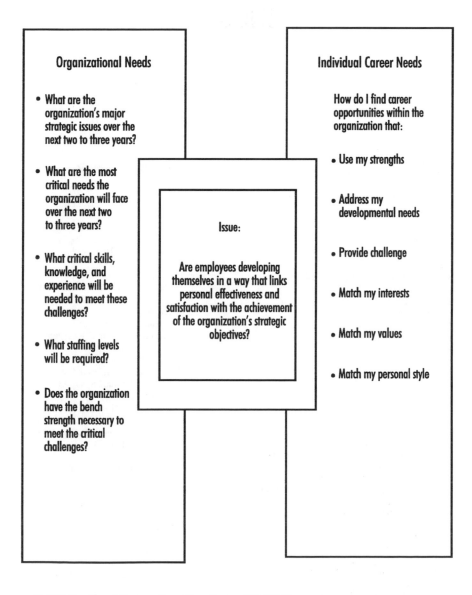

Organizational Needs

- What are the organization's major strategic issues over the next two to three years?

- What are the most critical needs the organization will face over the next two to three years?

- What critical skills, knowledge, and experience will be needed to meet these challenges?

- What staffing levels will be required?

- Does the organization have the bench strength necessary to meet the critical challenges?

Issue:

Are employees developing themselves in a way that links personal effectiveness and satisfaction with the achievement of the organization's strategic objectives?

Individual Career Needs

How do I find career opportunities within the organization that:

- Use my strengths

- Address my developmental needs

- Provide challenge

- Match my interests

- Match my values

- Match my personal style

Index

The authors welcome comments, feedback, and inquiries about this book and its contents, as well as related workshops and speaker engagements.

Please write us at:

Guerriero and Allen
Copter Productions
P. O. Box 81800
Chicago, IL 60681

or e-mail us at:

star@mail.mc.net

To order additional copies of this book please contact the order department of Lawrence Erlbaum Publishers, Inc., at:

phone:

1-800-9-BOOKS-9   (1-800-926-6579)

e-mail:

orders@erlbaum.com

online:

http://www.erlbaum.com